I'M YOUR MAN

Letters of the World's Most Ambitious Job Applicant

Sam Broadley

ISBN: 978-0-9957526-2-7

First published 2017. Second edition.

For Max.

May I inspire you as you inspire me.

CONTENTS

INTRODUCTION

Winston Churchill. Nelson Mandela. Martin Luther King. The Dalai Lama. Sam Broadley.

Everyone needs inspiration in their dwindling little lives. These great men are inspiration-providers.

If you're observant and can read (I certainly hope you *can* read, otherwise there's very little point in purchasing *any* book, let alone this one, and, indeed, you won't even be reading these words I'm writing; if you've got the audio version, listen on), you'll have noticed that Sam Broadley is the author of this book. That's me. And I may be the most inspirational of all the living men. At least on a par with Mr. Lama.

So why haven't you heard of me? (Unless you have, in which case, congratulations.) Why are all those others getting the plaudits while I sit here in my underwear writing an introduction to a book some people might buy? Simple: I inspire a smaller number of people – but massively so. The others are famous and get to inspire billions, but the quality of the inspiration is far more diluted. I prefer quality over quantity.

I say that, but I don't. I want quality *and* quantity. I *know* I can inspire every person on the planet (and those currently in outer space – they must not be forgotten), not just the few unimportant people in my life, like family and that. And when I do, it'll be inspiration of substance. Thick like a milkshake, not thin like squash.

*

I was 19 when I realised I was probably the best football coach in the land. That's why I applied for the role of England Manager. Fast-forward to my early-to-mid-twenties when I was doing menial jobs in soulless places like call centres, I looked around me at the buffoons and half-wits speaking to equally futile people of the public and thought to myself, *If only I'd have got the England job – I wouldn't be sitting here doing this rubbish; and think of the people I could've inspired with guaranteed footballing success.*

I could've got depressed. And I did. But then I thought, *No! Stop! Inspire yourself! And then get out there and inspire the world!!!* So I did. Well, I inspired myself.

What followed was a desperate quest to become everything I knew I could be. It was about getting to the top of the tree, the biggest of all the trees, because from the top of the tree, I can call my people, gather them in my forest and do what I do best – inspire. Inspire people to become great, to not accept their existing pointless versions of themselves.

And never have I had any interest in climbing the tree… it's about *jumping* to the top. To be Prime Minister, I want to just *become* Prime Minister, not go through all that nonsense of joining a party, serving people I don't care about, getting chosen to stand for election in some two-bit constituency, become a back-bencher, brown-nose my way into a Cabinet position, arrange a no-confidence vote in the existing Prime Minister, stand for Leader, *then* get the job… ugh, that could take *years*. And that goes for any job for which I've applied, whether it's President of the EU, James Bond or Pope. Or one of the many other roles I just *knew* I was perfect for. I'm just not prepared to wait and work for it. If I have to work my way up, people across the country and around the globe miss out on me while they wait. And that's not fair.

So this book is a journey from the age of 19 to 36, a journey that takes us through many application letters for jobs of the very highest standing in society. See the book as a careers lesson if you like, but more, see it – and me – as an inspiration. An inspiring man, I am, so make the most of me. Use me.

I was a nobody like you once. And now? Well, now, as I sit here in my bright-pink pants, I'm about to change your life. I reckon.

"Dreams are for sleepers... success comes to awake people. I'm an awake person. Wide awake. And success is just up the road, you'll see..."

Sam Broadley – self-proclaimed philosopher, pioneer and radical thinker.

Sam Broadley

████████████
████████████

Ipswich
Suffolk

██████████

15th October, 2000

Dear Adam Crozier,

I am writing to apply for the available position of **England Manager.**

I've become aware that in the last decade since the resignation of the beautiful Bobby Robson after the World Cup in 1990, there has been a lack of security with the comings and goings of no fewer than four different managers. By security, I don't mean an absence of safety for players, staff or fans; I'm sure you've got that nicely covered. I'm talking about the stability and future of our national game.

It is the general consensus, one I am sure you would go along with, that the job needs to be taken on with full, long-term commitment and dedication to help us to build for not only the World Cup in 2002 but major competitions for decades to come. We just cannot turn over managers like a farmer turns his fields. It's immoral.

I say immoral, but it's a harsh word. But I'm right. It's immoral to hire and fire managers, giving them barely enough time to pump up a football, even though it's their faults for being useless, and it's immoral to treat the fans with such contempt. You need to stop employing managers who you know have an excellent chance of failing. That's what's been happening and it's just not fair on them, nor the fans. It would be cruel to mention names, but in case you've forgotten who I'm talking about, I'll give you a clue: Graham T, Terry V, Glenn H. and Kevin Keegan.

My point is this: you need a man with a long-term plan. A man who will be at the helm for the next two decades and beyond. A man who can *guarantee* success throughout.

This is where I, a footballing fiend, come in.

A fiend?? A *fiend*??! Yes, a fiend! I haven't just misspelt 'friend'! What I mean is that I am fiendishly good at getting results. Devilishly good. I've proven it throughout my career, and I'll do anything it takes to win. You really don't want to know what I'd do…

Now's probably a good time to announce that I'm 19 years old. Yes, just a kid in all but the law. Well actually, no, I'm not a kid. I'm an adult, and a bloody good one, so don't even consider putting my application letter in the bin. That would be awful and a mistake (and not just because you should be shredding it for data protection purposes). Please listen. Or more specifically, read.

There are no shadows of doubt that I have the necessary credentials to fill this position and to set out to achieve the afore-mentioned target of winning every tournament for the next twenty years. I fully understand the national pressure on the person who takes this position, but I know that I have the mental strength to handle it and not be subjected to it. I don't feel pressure because I don't care about people. I just want to win.

Will you please stop thinking about my age? OK, let me put your mind at rest. You've undoubtedly assumed that I have no experience in football management. You'd be wrong, and I'd like to condemn you for making that assumption.

On the back of a wealth of playing experience at a high level throughout my youth, including for Ipswich Town School of Excellence, I went into management aged just 16. I knew I was ready. I'd failed to make it as a professional player (no fault of my own; I was definitely good enough, it's just my coaches foolishly didn't agree) and so it was time for me to give something back to the game. Well, I say give back, but the game has actually given me very little.

In any case, I knew it was time to take on a mighty team to propel forward into brilliance. And that's exactly what I did when I applied for and won the prestigious role of Manager of Martlesham Youth Under-7s. It was an honour to be given a chance at the club I grew up with. It can often be a big mistake for ex-players of a club to go back as manager – the esteem fans hold you in for what you achieved over those years can turn bitter overnight if you don't bring instant success as the boss. We've seen it happen time and again, especially at big clubs like Martlesham. They lose that hero status.

But that did not happen to me. Nope. I thrived on the challenge. I walked through the doors on the first day of training (there were no doors, actually; it was just across the pub car park and on to the green) and asserted my authority over those kids. They were awful. They could barely kick a ball, some of 'em. A total embarrassment. It was a long and arduous summer of pre-season as I sought to drag them into some kind of condition.

But do you know what? Despite the fact that half of them had only just learnt to walk, we went the whole year without a defeat. Mainly because they were too young to join a league, but still, stats are stats. It gave us great confidence going into the following season where we absolutely smashed it with a fourth-place finish. A sublime achievement, I'm sure you'll agree. There'll be plenty of managers out there who can only dream of such heights. It's exactly where Robson finished in '90. And when you consider we followed our achievement by finishing four from the top again the next year, well, why wouldn't you want to hire me? After such success with these boys, I feel I am ready to take that next step into international football management.

I have already set out a comprehensive plan as to the processes that will take place should you appoint me as England Manager. This plan has been drawn up as a result of a detailed ten-year log of the progression (or lack thereof) of our national team since 1990. I have noted where things have gone desperately wrong, where errors were made in player selection and poor tactical decisions in given games.

As an example, Ronald Koeman would never have been allowed to take that free kick to knock us out of the qualifying campaign for USA '94. It was obvious he was going to score so I'd have had someone kick his knee right on the side before he took it, just as he was running up to the ball. It might have resulted in a red card, but we'd most likely have got through and won the World Cup (if I was in charge, that is; I was only nine years old when the job become available after Bobby so I'd have done well to get it).

If you were to offer me an interview, I could without doubt persuade you in person that I am most definitely the right man for this incredibly prestigious job. So I look forward to meeting with you very soon so you can indeed offer me the job! And I will take it. Thank you.

Yours sincerely,

Sam Broadley

**THE FOOTBALL
ASSOCIATION**

25th October, 2000

Dear Mr. Broadley,

Thank you for your recent application for the position of National Team Coach.

As I am sure you can appreciate, we have been inundated with applications and are grateful for the interest and enthusiasm that the job has generated from people such as yourself.

The FA selection panel, working with Chief Executive Adam Crozier to find a successor to Kevin Keegan, has identified the criteria on which to judge the candidates. The criteria focus on evidence of their sustained football success as a coach/manager, their international experience, their standing among players, clubs and supporters and their tactical astuteness. Other criteria include integrity, handling of outside pressures, capacity to focus solely on the job, decision-making and communication skills, long-term commitment, ability to inspire a team and operate within it and their consistency of purpose.

A shortlist of three candidates has been drawn up by the selection panel, and Adam Crozier will be approaching each of these personally to discuss the position.

For the Executive Director

Sam Broadley

██████████████

██████████████

Ipswich
Suffolk
ENGLAND

████████

10th April, 2005

Dear Cardinals,

I am writing to formally apply for the currently available position of **Pope**.

I am a Roman Catholic. That is the first thing to say because I know it will impress you. At the very least, it will be a relief – what a catastrophic waste of everybody's time me going for the job if I wasn't!

Also, you may want to learn that I'm English. (You probably worked that out due to the fact that I'm writing in my native language (although I suppose I could be American or Canadian or Australian or New Zealandan. Ah, actually, scrap that – I've just seen I put 'ENGLAND' in my address at the top of the letter so you already know (if you read it)!).)

It's fair to say I would not class myself as having lived a Catholic life exactly 'by the book' to date. But who has? Even you good men have had your moments of debauchery, I'm sure! Rascals! But like you, I have always lived my life with God as my guidance and have learned from mistakes and sins. That's the good thing about this religion – you know you'll get forgiven in the end for anything you do as long as you admit it!!!

But I don't say that lightly. I know it does not mean I can go ahead and do bad things knowing in advance that I'm doing wrong and think God will forgive me. It's about committing sins *spontaneously* or *accidentally*. Those are the times when God will look upon me and think, *You know what? He's done wrong, it was a mistake, he's very sorry, I will let it go and move on.* And I commend Him for that. It takes a big man to forgive and forget, and they don't come much bigger than Him.

It is difficult for people, though, to really know what is right and wrong in this day and age. We're not just talking about eating an apple anymore. Sure, we're not an amoral species, but there are so many grey areas. For example, getting drunk is frowned upon, yet the Church teaches us to drink wine as a tribute to Jesus. But how much is too much? Can I drink His blood all day and get wasted, knowing that I'm drinking the holiest alcohol in the universe? Or it is more about my behaviour once I've been drinking? Am I allowed to talk to girls or only if I intend to marry them? Can I dance at the disco?

These are the sorts of questions people have to wrestle with every waking day, and it's not fair. Why can't we have more clarity? That's what the new Pope needs to deliver. The rules need to be clear like tracing paper. He needs to get out there and tell his people, "YES, you can drink; YES, you can dance; YES you can talk to girls, although I urge you to marry them swiftly because you can't touch them until you do, otherwise you will go to Hell, and then when you do wed, you must never, ever, *ever* use contraception because that is preventing the creation of life, and thinking about it, you must have intercourse as often as you are physically capable of with your wife because not doing is also preventing the creation of life and you will go to Hell if you don't, and I don't care if you have to go to work or take your existing twenty-four children to school or walk the dog, you must, *must*, must get back into bed with her at even the slightest tingle 'down there', because if you prevent the creation of as many lives as you are physically capable of producing, you will go to Hell for all eternity, and don't you forget it. And it doesn't matter if the world is totally overrun with human beings, *that's* the Catholic way. The *right* way, apparently. Your new man needs to spread that vital message.

This is where I, a papal prince, come in.

Not an official prince, but I am prince-like. It's the way I carry myself. It's like a natural aura I give off that makes people question the colour of my blood (whether or not it's blue, I mean). Prince is probably not enough to describe me. More of a king. That feels a bit much; I am but a humble fellow, but it's how my people feel. I don't wear a crown, mainly because I'm not actual royalty. Some people respect me as if I'm angelic so I sometimes wear a halo.

And that brings me to the 'papal' bit of my self-description. I'm basically *designed* to be Pope. I was born to play the role. It's a bit like the Buddhists knowing who their Dalai Lama is from a very early age. People always had this feeling about me when I was growing up because of the way I used to pray, almost as if I was having a full-on conversation with God rather than the one-way chats everyone else experiences.

People have always come to me as their beacon of hope. I am their guidance during times of sadness, confusion, strife. They depart full of joy, clarity, life (essentially the opposite of whatever they come to me with, unless they arrive with something positive, then it's more of the same).

And I'm not talking about simply close family members here.

It's extended family as well. And some friends. So if you scale it up worldwide, well, that's a world's worth of people I can touch (emotionally; let's not go there, Catholics…).

So when I say I'm a *papal* prince, I mean that I have all the hallmarks of a Pope-in-waiting. Anyone who meets me or feels my presence knows it. You're probably feeling me now. Or you at least want to. You certainly will when you meet me. And I'll let you.

Once you've met me and felt me, I have no doubt in the world that I'll get your vote. But just to show you what I'm about and how I intend to attract people to the Church and the ways of God, I'll show you how I will be doing just that.

First, I will be entering *Big Brother*. This is a hugely popular television show here in Britain whereby contestants live in a house together for several weeks, playing games and talking nonsense, and the public vote individuals to be evicted every now and again. Eventually, there is one person left standing who is crowned the winner. During my time in the house, I will, thanks to my immense powers of communication and manipulation, convert the contestants to a life of Catholicism and all the fun that goes with it, and in turn do exactly the same to the millions of viewers. I'll also win the show. I'm a winner like that.

So that's my homeland taken care of. Next it's my continent, Europe, where England is. And I'll be conquering it by entering the Eurovision Song Contest. I have a couple of fantastic songs lined up. One is called *Pope! In the Name of Love…* and the other is *Papal Does Preach*. Both have fabulous party rhythms that will get the crowd going and the viewers at home will be going mad round their living rooms! But more than that, my songs have subliminal messages to convert people to my way of thinking. Again, I expect to win the competition. I'd be happy to sing these songs for you with my angelic voice during the interview process if you'd like. I reckon afterwards, you'll be more Catholic than you were before!!!

As for the world stage, well, have I got something special in store for you or what?! At first, I was going to see if I could get God to appear on my balcony with me. Goodness, that would draw in the crowds! But then I decided I didn't want to be upstaged so I will leave that for later down the road.

Instead, I'm going to perform a miracle. And not just any old miracle that any old saint can do. No. Anyone can cure someone of an incurable illness. I want to go bigger.

I will rid the world of all sin.

I told you I was going big! But how will I do it? Simple: by making everything that is a sin *no longer a sin*. "RIDICULOUS!" I hear you shout in anger. But no, not ridiculous when you really think about it, so I'd ask you not to jump to conclusions like that and just hear me out.

My thinking is that by the time I have changed the rules on sinning (and don't worry, I'll be running it by God first; I'm not so arrogant as to think I can make that decision alone), I will have conquered such a chunk of the world with my ideas, be worshipped so intensely by people, vast swathes will be living by my every word. Even those from other religions will listen and act.

By the time I make the announcement that literally *anything* people want to do, they *can* do, I will basically be running the world. Not through law, but *influence*. I will say that in the eyes of God, from this day forward, anything goes. But I will *urge* them to think about whether they actually *want* to do those things they are now entirely welcome to do, notwithstanding the laws of their lands. Do they really *want* to hurt that person? Do they really *want* to steal that watch? Do they really *want* to sleep with their neighbour's wife? Despite their almost overwhelming natural desire to do those things, their own *consciences* (which I now control, don't forget) will stop people from doing them. They won't actually *want* to. So no longer are good people *not* doing bad things only so they don't get in trouble with God, they're being good because they *feel good being good*. And the naturally bad people are no longer doing bad because I have made them *good*! *That's* the profound effect I will have on all the billions of people on our planet.

Think what this will do everywhere. If people aren't doing bad things, *good* things are being done in their place. Or at least neutral. There'll be no need for law enforcement. No need for armies. No need for security guards or traffic wardens. Alright, a massive number of people working in public services will be out of a job, but so what? Not my problem. They'll have to look for something else. And don't be thinking it'll mean they'll turn to a life of crime in their desperation – I own their minds now, remember…!

I'm aware, by the way, that this would not technically be performing a miracle. But it's bloody close! And far more of an impact, that is for sure. What *good* it will bring to our world. Finally, our species can prosper! And it gives God a break from having to forgive all those sins all the time!!!

I am currently in employment within the sales sector, selling travel insurance (so if you ever need a quote, you know where to come!). But I have so much more to offer than this drivel. I have all the above to offer. Plus I'm sick of hearing about other people's holidays all day every day. It's about time I did some travelling, and what better way to do so than as Pope.

The work our great John Paul did should be seen as just the beginning of immensity. From here, I can develop upon the foundations this fine man built. I am young. 24, to be precise to the nearest year. I have no interest in taking this position in my 60s or 70s. I'm impatient, for one thing. And although the world will be singing from my hymn sheet in a matter of weeks, I really want to be Pope for a bloody long time. I am at the absolute perfect age to take on this mammoth role.

You will have a number of candidates in mind, most likely among yourselves as cardinals. But I challenge you to look beyond the boundaries of the old boys' club and vote for someone like myself who is willing to devote his life to the cause in accordance with God and all He and I wish to achieve. Be brave. God likes bravery.

I look forward to meeting with you soon so that I can sing my way into your glorious hearts.

Yours faithfully,

Sam Broadley

Sam Broadley

██████████
██████████
Ipswich
Suffolk
██████████

17th May, 2006

Dear Mr. David Sheepshanks,

I am writing to formally apply for the currently vacant position of **Manager** of Ipswich Town FC.

I am a 25-year-old player, coach and manager. A brief history: my playing career began at the age of eight. From there I represented Suffolk County throughout my teen years, and I played for the School of Excellence at Ipswich Town for three seasons until the age of 16, at which point I was released. Yes – released. By you. You kicked me out. Or more specifically, George Burley did. Or more specifically still, one of the coaches. Whoever it was, I was devastated and at a loss to understand what the club I loved had done to me. I felt violated.

I accepted that my ability as a player fell short of the required standard of a professional, so I turned my hand to coaching (whilst still playing to a high standard). I moved into a management position with Martlesham Youth Under-7s, whom I coached for three years. Despite my young age, I found this to be my calling. To watch the children develop under my guidance from complete newcomers to the game to fine young footballers was a tremendous achievement.

In 2000, I went to Lincoln University and carried on my playing and coaching. I represented the 1st team and won Player of the Year in 2002. It was now I realised that, actually, I *was* good enough to be a pro and that you and your Ipswich Town cronies had made a seriously grave error. Especially now you'd been relegated from the Premier League! When that happened, I didn't know whether to laugh or cry, so I did both.

I was employed for a brief spell by Ipswich Town as a Community Coach in the summer of 2002. During this time, I seriously contemplated corrupting the club from the inside because of what you'd done to me, or at least give the kids some bad coaching. But just as I wouldn't be able to publicly share any naked pictures of any given ex-girlfriend, even though I would really, really, really love to get revenge for being dumped by text (isn't that just so cowardly?), I just couldn't do it because love is deep-rooted. I just love this club, love it like a lover, and that is why you, Sir, hold this letter in your hands.

I am sure that you will be somewhat concerned at what could possibly be perceived as my limited coaching and management experience at the highest levels. My response to this would be that I know I have the capability, confidence and that touch of what I call 'positive arrogance' to be a huge success in the job.

You'll be reassured to know that I am currently working towards my Level One coaching badge. That can only give you confidence, knowing that I am committed to becoming qualified in what I want to do. And to think I've already had such success *without* the qualifications! To try and imagine what I could achieve *with* the all the badges is just scary! Don't miss out and let that raw talent go to waste or, worse still, Norwich! (That's a genuine threat.)

I challenge you, Sheepy, to overlook my age and relatively minimal experience and see that there is huge potential for success in taking someone with youth, enthusiasm and an abundance of skill, as well as a character who naturally acquires respect from colleagues. I can take this club forward to the level at which it should be competing, undoubted.

It is of course difficult to prove my worth in writing; a face-to-face interview would open your eyes, I'm sure. My drive and ideas will intrigue you and enthuse you, astound and excite you. Be sure that my managerial prowess is not to be sniffed at. I can turn average players into good players, good players into great players, develop young players and re-enthuse players lacking confidence; all this to improve as a collective unit and move in the same direction.

I have the style of George Burley and the guile of Bobby Robson.

As a fan, I am aware there has been collective disappointment that we have not lately been seeing the type of exciting and dictating football we have enjoyed for the past decade. We need these days to return. I know how to find them – by looking backwards. I am a backward-thinker.

I am wary of people who talk a good game, and that is how I may have come across, but hopefully, I have done enough to arouse you, enough for you to wish to meet me face-to-face. I am aware that you would be taking a gamble with me (in your eyes, not mine; I *know* I'm the best you can get), therefore I am happy to work alongside established names for a while to prove my worth. But only on my terms, they being that I am in charge, not them. I may or may not keep them on my payroll, they ought to be aware. It is up to them to impress me, not me them. Alright? (I love assertive behaviour!)

My love for Ipswich Town FC cannot be denied. Yes, I have scars that will never heal, but in time and with me back at the heart of the club, I feel we can all move on and taste success. Not just taste, but *eat* it. And I promise to never consider corrupting the club again.

I look forward to hearing from you very soon indeed.

Yours sincerely and all my love,

Sam Broadley

12th June, 2006

Dear Sam,

Thank you for your recent application for the position of Manager at Ipswich Town Football Club. However, we regret to advise that you have been unsuccessful on this occasion.

After an extensive interview process, you will know that we have made an internal appointment of Jim Magilton with Bryan Clug assisting him as First Team Coach.

May I wish you the best of luck for the future and thank you for your interest.

With best wishes,

Yours sincerely,

David Sheepshanks
Chairman

Sam Broadley

██████████
██████████

Ipswich

Suffolk

██████████

9th October, 2006

Dear Delia Smith,

I am writing to formally apply for the available position of **Manager** of Norwich City FC.

Please read these things about me. My dream as a youngster was to become a professional player, the best left-back the nation has ever seen. My first experience with a professional club was at 13 when I had a lengthy trial with Cambridge United. It was here that I really realised that I could become something special. Unfortunately, they did not agree.

I soon transferred to my hometown club, Ipswich Town (please don't hold this against me when considering my application). I spent three wonderful years here, playing alongside great names such as Titus Bramble and Keiron Dyer. I had such confidence in my ability, and I believed I was destined for big things. I felt that I needed the game, but equally, the game needed me. Unfortunately, Town did not agree. I was unsuccessful, not through a lack of ability, but mainly an addiction to food, any food.

At 16, I accepted my chance as a player was over, so I moved into management. I took charge of my local village team, Martlesham Youth Under-7s. I was there for three years, and my success was phenomenal. The progress the boys made under my guidance was nothing short of remarkable. I'd found my calling in life.

I went on to become a student (of sorts) at Lincoln University and continued both my playing and coaching careers. My coaching in particular really took off, helping the first team to second spot in the league against long odds – success equivalent to Norwich City winning promotion this season. (Good luck with that if you don't hire me.)

With my confidence buzzing, I felt I was ready to take the next step on the road to managerial stardom, so I applied for the England job after Kevin Keegan's departure. Sadly, the FA decided that it was better to instate a passionless foreigner than someone like myself. I often wonder if they look back and secretly regret not giving a fresh-faced young man like me the chance.

This was only a minor setback. I was happy to work hard at my game and learn my trade. After further success with Lincoln University, I went on to coach a local Under-14s team here in Ipswich, helping to turn a bunch of no-hopers into league survival candidates. Again, I was successful, staying up on the last day of the season. Maybe I could've done the same for Norwich City had I have been in charge against Fulham two years ago…

This success led me to think seriously again at having a stab at the pro leagues, and when my dream job came up at my beloved Ipswich Town, I jumped at the chance to apply. For a man who dreamt for years as a child to play for the club he worshipped, this was a big opportunity for me to be a part of the set-up and turn dreams into reality, change the fortunes of the club and hit the big-time whilst looking down on our lowly neighbours languishing in the lower leagues. I know that I have the managerial prowess to turn any club around, but when you couple that ability with love in its purest form, stronger than even that for my own family, one can only triumph.

However, the club I have followed since God was a boy let me down. As much as I love Magic Jim Magilton (and I do), he has less managerial experience than me. That is a fact. I laid out my plans to the club in a letter, told them of the strategies I would implement to turn the club and players' careers around and win the fans over.

They didn't even invite me for an interview.

As a result, I am writing to you. Although my love for Town can never die, I am bitter and feel I need to teach them a lesson, and what better way than to travel 50 miles down the A140 to take charge of their fierce rivals and show them how to really run a club. I would love nothing more than to join your club as manager, do the double over Town, leapfrog them in the league table in weeks, win promotion to the Premiership and challenge for the title within two years!

Obviously, I am unknown to you and much of the footballing world. There will be other more established names you will be considering. But don't forget that the bigger names don't always match their reputations. Sometimes, they demand big money but don't win football matches. I win football matches.

I challenge you, Ms Smith, to cook up a big dish of controversy and introduce this delicious 25-year-old lamb to your club. On your plate, you will have a boy with all the ingredients to prepare Norwich City for a banquet of success for many years to come. The style of football I will instil into all my players will be tasty, creating a feast of entertainment for all our guests at Carrot Road. Fans will go away feeling satisfied but hungry for more.

Let me be the one to come in and whet the fans' appetites. Let me be the one to come in and spice up the players' careers. Let me be the one to feed those supporters being starved of success. Consider me and no-one at Norwich City Football Club will go hungry.

I look forward to meeting you and presenting you with my ideas in full to smash those southern Tractors!

Yours sincerely,

Sam Broadley

DELIA SMITH

Norwich City Football Club

October, 2006

Dear Sam Broadley,

Thank you for your recent letter to Delia Smith.

Delia is currently away, but I will forward your correspondence when she returns.

Kind regards,

████████

Norwich City Football Club

October, 2006

Dear Sam,

Thank you for your recent letter to Delia Smith offering your services as Manager at Norwich City Football Club.

No doubt you will have followed events recently at Carrow Road. I hope you approve of the decisions that have been made.

Thank you once again for your interest in Norwich City Football Club.

On the ball City!

Sam Broadley

██████████

██████████

Norwich

Norfolk

██████████

16th May, 2007

Dear Rt. Hon. Ms Hazel Blears,

I am writing to formally apply for the soon-to-be-available position of Labour Party **Leader / Prime Minister**.

With Tony Blair vacating the post after ten years of service to our country, he leaves behind a legacy which includes profound work in resolving the Northern Ireland conflict, weighty efforts in improving education and perhaps a highly controversial War On Terror.

My personal view of Mr. Blair's tenure is one of general satisfaction, perhaps 70% so, but for me that's 30% that could've been better. With just three years until the next General Election, it is imperative we improve.

This is where I, a Labour lover, come in.

I am 26-years-old. Yes, only 26 but running for leadership. But before you condemn this letter to the blades of the shredder or consign it to the 'nutter' pile, please consider the advancements I will make on the good work of Tony Blair and his Cabinet, and the plan of innovation I have in place to ensure another ten years of power. There are many things we need to do.

A quick joke: Where did Saddam keep his CDs? In a rack! (Iraq... get it?!). Ahem. Just a little joke there to break the ice on a tense subject.

The Iraq war is without doubt the biggest military event since World War II. Whilst the principle of the invasion of Iraq was one I utterly agreed with, the subsequent plan to revive the country's stability and install a freestanding democracy was messy, at best. We could talk all day of the reasons for why, but I am a forward-thinker, and should you consider me for the position of Labour Leader, you'll see just how I plan on turning it all around in Iraq. Believe me, it's not to be missed. Suffice to say it's all the Yanks' fault, we were bullied into it, but we've come out mentally stronger. Our Boys are coming home.

You will undoubtedly be considering other more established names to take over the leadership from Mr. Blair. In fact, it seems Gordon Brown, who, as Chancellor, has worked wonders in stabilising and strengthening our economy, is poised to take over automatically. Other names have been loosely thrown into the hat: John Reid and Charles Clarke, to name but two. But whilst they are highly regarded among peers, they fail to have the one thing that really sells to a public: sex appeal.

It's true that sex sells. Think of the adverts on television. How do Cadbury's sell Flakes? With a sexy woman sucking provocatively on the chocolatey stick. What about the Dairy Milk deliveries from the mysterious sexy man? And how does Renault sell its cars? The sexy 'Nicole-Papa' storyline. It's time to turn politics around and make it sexy!

As the catwalk model that I am (and I am), I can offer this to you, the Labour Party. Not only do I have the brains, confidence and drive to take this party well into the 21st century, it's true I have the sex appeal to go with it. I suppose I am just one of the lucky ones. I am but a modest man, but I can see the tabloid headlines now…

SEXABLE SAM FOR PRIME MINISTER!

Don't scoff at this. Think about it logically. The British public are mugs. They'll buy anything. That's why credit card companies are richer than a Tea biscuit. Get the voters excited about Sexy Sam Broadley, the sexual fledgling who gets whisked in like a whirlwind to change the face of Britain, the man who could charm the trousers off John Major and the peas off his plate, oozing sex appeal like a younger, better-looking Blair (I can bring plenty of my own babes, by the way). They won't be thinking politics, they'll just want me!

Obviously, looks aren't everything. The politics is what we need to concentrate on; it's serious business. But my point is this: once the public has gone weak at the knees over the hot new Labour leader, the opinion polls start to turn in our favour thanks to blind shallowness, *then* we start concentrating on policies and what we can really offer the country. Pop star looks can only take us so far, I know that. But this face can get us the positive attention we need, and then with voters on our side once more, the hard work of keeping them can really begin.

It's also true that the number of people voting these days has dwindled to pathetic levels. It's either because they think all parties are rubbish and therefore there is no point in voting, or they just have zero interest in politics. I love Labour and like to think a lot of fellow countrymen (and women; equality is so important to me) do too, so I'm going for the second one.

With record numbers failing to vote in elections, it's time to get the new generations involved, appeal to the kids. It's time to turn their heads, then get *in* their heads.

No doubt you're thinking to yourself, "Well, what are Sexable

Sam's political credentials?" And rightly so. Well, I will admit my experience of Parliament is at best, limited, and at worst, non-existent. Probably closer to the latter, in all honesty. Although I have visited Parliament. I saw the outside. A fine building.

But I want you to know that I am an avid watcher of Question Time. Every Thursday evening at 10.35pm without fail, there I am in front of the telly, nodding and clapping at every sensible comment or boiling with anger and shaking a fist at some fat, farcical politician who doesn't know his face from his backside (sometimes I don't know with them either; horrendous lack of sex appeal).

My knowledge and sense of logic on that show would be plain for all to see should I make an appearance. And because I have the common touch with people, I would not be too big, even as Prime Minister, to grace the Question Time panel – as a regular fixture should the BBC wish so. I wonder if the viewing figures would quadruple. Time will tell.

I should also point out that my current vocation is as a Crime Investigator for Norfolk Constabulary. I've seen all sorts. I'm sure you can appreciate that I cannot go into any detail, but believe me, with the office politics going on here, I am more than ready to take the next step and become Prime Minister.

You will see I've included two pictures of myself. They are to complement my good points in the different scenarios of modern politics. One is of me looking sharp and meaning business (Prime Minister's Questions?), the other of me in a typical modelling pose (Labour PR photo shoot?). Have a bit of fun and see if you can work out which one's which. I'll give you the correct answer when we meet.

Please accept this application in the serious manner in which it is written. I truly believe I have all the attributes to make an excellent Prime Minister, and I would love this to be with the Labour party.

If you are in doubt over my credibility to be Leader, think of the PR. We'll make the front page for sure!!!

I look forward to meeting you face-to-face and working together over the coming years to make this country a Laborious one (in a good way; just a play on words, really).

Yours sincerely,

Sam Broadley

Sam Broadley

██████████████

██████████████

Norwich

Norfolk

██████████

25th July, 2007

Dear *Thomas the Tank Engine* owners,

I am writing to formally apply for the position of **Narrator** for *Thomas the Tank Engine.*

I understand that, by applying, I am attempting to fill some rather impressive boots. Ringo Starr is obviously one of the biggest names to come out of the cartoon industry, and it would be a true honour to follow in his footsteps and take on the prestigious job of continuing the vocal life of Britain's favourite train.

Thomas was certainly my favourite train. I can recall watching episodes with such joy, over and over. I am told that, as a child, I was never happier than when sat in front of the telly, swaying to the catchy theme tune (which I can still, to this day, accurately sing for you) and becoming actively enthralled by Thomas's latest capers.

Despite my sincere fondness for Thomas, my love for trains in general never really bloomed. In fact, I loathe them. I have yet to obtain my driving licence, and so my reliance on the rail network to get me cross-country to see friends is plain to see, but I cannot form any kind of positive relationship with the train – electric, steam or otherwise.

I think my abhorrence comes from years of high prices, delays and lack of general good service. Too many times I have paid a good chunk of my weekly wage for a seat on a train, which has been delayed for sometimes two hours, while platform staff display little-to-no sympathy, and once the train has finally chugged in (showing no sign of urgency as it arrives, the slow chugs whispering like rhythmic, arrogant taunts), I then find the seat I paid good money for has been taken by some four-eyed, grey suit-wearing, high-flying City git tapping away on his 'laptop', whilst donning one of those laughable 'earpieces' for his 'mobile phone'. I could ask him for my seat which I reserved, but usually they are better people than me and I get intimidated, so I tend to just stand between carriages.

My apologies for my little rant there. I sometimes get a little worked up. I just don't like the idea of fat-cats making unjustifiably high sums of money and laughing at my expense.

My distaste for the rail should of course not affect my application to become the voice of old Thomas. My assumption is that knowledge and love of the railway network is hardly a prerequisite for the role. One should be judged on one's talents as a performer, as an entertainer, and one's ability to take TtTE into a new and wonderful era.

This is where I, a vocal marvel, come in.

I've been told I have a lovely voice. "Honest", one called it. "Inspiring", said another. Some people even say sexy. Perhaps that's foolish, I don't know. I'm rather modest when it comes to judging myself; I prefer to let others tell me how great I am.

What I do know about my vocal talents is that I am not a one-trick pony. I have many strings to my bow. I have a performing background, playing an array of roles, therefore I have developed a range of voices, accents and impressions. Jesus Christ, Mafia Don,

German sailor, woman and a gay, to name but five I've covered (in performance). You don't get much more varied than that.

Accents is really where I shine. Brummie, Yorkshire, Norfolk (I'm from Suffolk – they differ enormously), Londoner, Aussie, Northern Irish, German (broken English), South African, Texan – you name it, I can (probably) do it. I'd have to say that Australian is probably my preferred and most perfected accent. I remember once having a conversation with a girl outside a nightclub for an hour and ten minutes, talking of my life in Australia, how I was born and raised in Darwin and had come to Pomme-Land for my love of the English girls. For *her*. She fell for it and she was mine.

When it comes to impressions, Sinn Fein Nationalist Party leader Gerry Adams is a personal favourite (the impression, not him, his party or his values). However, due to the current political climate, I only give sporadic public performances of this particular talent. More light-hearted impressions include Alan Partridge, Phil Mitchell and my mum's friend Suzanne.

While you will no doubt be considering more established names to take on this fabulous job (it's not a job), I would remind you that Ringo Starr was not an actor. He was the drummer from the famous pop band *The Beatles*. And a bloody good one. Despite his background being in music, you gave him the chance to prove his worth as an actor – and he did just that. A wonderful success story, and he can be proud of his stint as the voice of Thomas.

I can offer you a similar level of talent – just not the brand name to go with it. But this can be developed. You will not be disappointed in what I have to offer – and neither will our audience. My unique sounds will enthuse you and excite you, enthral you and enchant you.

Let me pick you up and let's dance and ride all the way to Seventh Heaven, stopping at Happidom, Thrillville, Savvy Street, Ecstasy Way, Choochoo Avenue, finally arriving at Seventh Heaven.

I look forward to hearing from you and taking Thomas, his friends and our children to a new level of chuffing magic.

Yours faithfully,

Sam Broadley

Sam Broadley

█████████████

█████████████

Norwich
Norfolk

████████████

18th October, 2007

Dear Mr. Simon Hughes,

I am writing to formally apply for the currently available position of **Leader** of the Liberal Democrats.

Before discussing my own credentials for becoming your leader, I would firstly like to pay homage to the great Rt. Hon. Sir Menzies Campbell CBE QC. Ming, as he likes to be called, brought a certain charm to your lot. With the Lib Dems seemingly going nowhere and riddled with scandal, up stepped the man himself to stabilise the party, establish a solid structure and some professionalism (at last) and restore the backbone that makes the Lib Dems stand so tall. Well, taller than Grumpy, Sneezy and Dopey, at least.

What a shame, though, that this great nation has become so preoccupied with age. Old Minger is 66 years old, as I'm sure you're aware, being president of the party and all. For me, 66 is the new 36 (although to scale, at 26, that would make me the new -6). When people speak of him appearing tired and worn, I say to them, "I think you'd look pretty knackered if you were an Olympic runner", as he was in his younger days. I also remind people of the scientific and medical advances we continue to make daily. Who's to say that, with the right combination of exercise, medicine and good old hearty desire, Mr. Campbell could not have lead us well into his 90s, or maybe even 100s? (Some think he already has.)

47

Despite my hurt at the departure of such an iconic man, I am a positive person and I am determined to seek pluses from this, on the face of it, cheerless turn of events. The press think Ming is too old. Well let's go the other way: let's whisk in a whirlwind whippersnapper!

This is where I, a vivacious, democratic demon, come in.

Again, I am 26 and look younger. Yes, 40 years Ming's junior. I hope my senses are wrong, Mr. Hughes. I am not a psychic nor a mind-reader and never likely to be, but I hope I did not just hear you thinking, *That's ridiculous, 26 is way too young to lead this party.* (Probably not because you're not reading this as I'm writing it.) As a liberal man and with the prejudice the party has seen of late, I hope you are not being ageist.

My belief is that I am at the optimum age. Not just my belief – it's a fact. Think about this logically. 26 means my youth is behind me. No more school, no college. No tantrums, no more adolescent outbursts. I am well into adulthood – and I'm thriving on it. I have been a grown-up for long enough now to know stuff about the world. I feel wise. I know what's right, I know what's wrong. I know what needs changing, I know what needs innovating. I'm a *man*.

26 means I have decades of service to give. As leader, I am willing to give myself entirely to the party, to dedicate my whole life (apart from the bit I've already had) to the Liberal Democrats and Great Britain. I aim to live 'til I'm at least 100, so that's a minimum of 74 years of service. Surely a record in the making.

For me, top-level success in politics is to possess the ultimate logical train of thought, to have thoroughly unblinkered vision and prudent foresight, to own the ability to strike a sound balance to maintain the equilibrium of the many intertwining tightropes of society. You won't find anyone more logically balanced than me, of that I can assure you.

I'd like to be honest with you from the outset, Mr. Hughes. When former Prime Minister Tony Blair left office, I applied to step into his vacant shoes. Please can I ask you not to let this hinder my application. The reason I applied to Labour was because I felt Mr. Blair had made some grave errors which I needed to radically rectify. I'm not one for slating rivals; it's unprofessional. However, I think he knows himself that his tenure was littered with monumentally bad decisions that have left this country in a state of turmoil. I have a distinct belief in my ability to run this country, and although Labour is not my choice of party, I felt compelled to get in as soon as I could and set about righting his wrongs.

The good news for you, though, is that my application was not accepted. In fact, they did not even reply to my letter, which, for me, reinforces their conscious detraction from their public. In hindsight, I am pleased they did not employ me. I am a Liberal, Mr. Hughes. Please know that. I know what I can bring to the table, and in the event of a formal face-to-face interview, I can promise you that the room will be rife with electric excitement.

We must remember that we have literally no chance of getting in power. Of that there is no doubt. Honestly, zero. Obviously. But that's not to put us down. We are a special party and we can go somewhere. Not down, because it's almost impossible to go much lower. But certainly a slight incline from horizontal, at the very least. We've got to be ambitious like that. Labour and the Tories are just too good for us, we know that.

But with me at the helm, we can achieve those lofty ambitions of some improvement! And with at least 74 years ahead of me to achieve it, what a chance we have! Come on, we can do this!!!

I look forward to hearing from you and, all being well, meeting you very soon.

Yours sincerely,

Sam Broadley

PS: I'm so liberal, I'll turn up to the interview naked if you like.

Sam Broadley

██████████
██████████

Ipswich
Suffolk

██████████

19th September, 2008

Dear Channel 4,

After the news that Des O'Connor is sensationally quitting the show, I am writing to formally apply for the forthcoming available position of **Presenter** of *Countdown*.

A bit about myself: I am 27 years old and work as a recruitment consultant. The job is highly challenging and one I am proud to be succeeding in, but for me, it's too much like hard work so my future lies in television.

I have been a fan of the show since God was but a little boy, or, more specifically, I was a little boy, right from the moment I could read. Day in, day out, I would sit there with my pen and paper, write down the letters as they came out and play along with the contestants. I would never even allow myself more time than the allotted 30 seconds, even though the letters stayed on the screen way longer. If I was to beat the contestants, it was to be done fairly. I would only be cheating myself. I am not a cheat.

Sadly, I never won. Not once. I'm honest to admit I was less than average. I could spell and I could write, but give me nine jumbled up letters and ask me to find some words and I was in a whole world of trouble.

And we haven't even discussed numbers.

But of course, the ability to play the game is not a prerequisite to present the show. I think it is fair to say that the legendary Richard Whiteley was not the most gifted with words or numbers, by his own admission. His successor, the charming Des Lynam, the same. Ditto Des O'Connor. Not the brightest. This is why we have Carol Vorderman and Dictionary Corner. If the contestants can't do it, they will.

But why pick me? Well, I would like you to consider a new approach. You will know better than me, I'm sure, but I would imagine the bulk of your viewers will be the pensioners, especially if your studio audience is anything to go by. I've seen younger veterans of the Boer War.

Have you ever thought of appealing to a wider audience? Targeting the young as well as the not-so? I'd like to bring a fresh impetus to the show. I am young and look younger. I carry with me the obvious qualities a young man can bring (energy, enthusiasm, a future), whilst retaining the intrinsic worth and charm of Richard, Des and Des.

Consider this: by hiring me as Presenter, I would be secretly helping thousands of college and university students up and down the country who are too lazy to study to recapture the fresh energy and vigour that drove them to further their education in the first place. But how?

Friends close to me will speak of my humble ways, but I think it's fair to say I am not unattractive. No way. Hell, no. Once word gets round of the 'eye candy' (person with good looks) now presenting the show, we will have attracted a new share of the market – students who don't study. Trust me, from personal experience, there are plenty of these.

I, myself, was once a lazy student. Yes, it's true. I know you don't believe it having witnessed my energy levels and determination to succeed (I am aware we have never met and therefore you have yet to actually witness this – I am simply anticipating your reaction of astonishment).

Location: University of Lincoln, Lincoln, Lincolnshire. After an incident one cold October morn of 2000 (the year), which I'd prefer not to discuss, it was feared (by myself) that I had developed agoraphobia (a fear of the outdoors). It was a frightful time in my life. I stayed indoors for days and days, eating takeaways, drinking beer and playing *Pro Evolution Soccer* on the PlayStation (the first edition – there have been eight further) and *Championship Manager* (a football fantasy game for the PC where you manage your own football club and see how far you can take them). These were played with my friend Jonah (not his real name). He did not have any phobias. I suspect that he understood my problems and wished to stay with me to work through my difficult time and so sacrificed many, many lectures. Friends like that are hard to come by.

Astonishingly, against the odds and all predictions, it actually turned out I did *not* have agoraphobia! I found this out only by chance. One day, I had finally decided that enough was enough and I could not live life like this. It was time for the nurse's intervention. Approximately six minutes into my eight-minute walk to the surgery, I suddenly realised I was OUTSIDE and had thought nothing of it! I had inadvertently proven to myself that I was *not* an agoraphobic!! YES!!!

Despite having no need to visit the nurse, I carried on with my journey (she was attractive; my friend kissed her once). We discussed at length the problems I'd had over recent days (47 of them). After prolonged analysis, the nurse's conclusion was that, back in October, I had found a lecture particularly difficult (to stay awake in) and had subconsciously given myself a condition which would enable me to stay indoors, consume alcohol and grease-ridden food whilst playing sports-related computer games every day instead of studying for a degree in a subject I had little-to-no interest in. She understood but advised me to return to studies. She's a good nurse. Wise and respected.

I ignored her advice.

So what was the point in offering you a snippet of my medical history? Well, I'm just giving you an example of the many reasons students find themselves away from the lecture theatres, neglecting their all-important readings. The fact is that these young adults face issues of motivation, lacking understanding that they are capable people who once aspired to be something but have forgotten all about it.

The thousands of students absent from class watch rubbish daytime television. But probably not *Countdown*. With Sam "The Face" Broadley in the Chair, what will happen is this: the young viewership will snowball as knowledge of "The Face"'s premiership travels with tens of thousands tuning in every day. As more students watch, they watch together. If they watch together, they become competitive. As the competition grows, the effort they put in to find the best words (or ones with the most number of letters) increases. Students then realise they have talents that had laid not only dormant but undiscovered for years.

Suddenly, these students have a new zest for life. They realise that the challenge of finding words of one-to-nine letters is driving them to succeed, to out-wit fellow students, to be the best. We will find that with this newly-rediscovered energy comes motivation to get back into the classroom (not before recording *Countdown*) and prove to themselves, their families and their friends that they can succeed and be the best.

What a result this will be for the country. Increased exam results and degree scores, a new generation of young professionals with increased confidence and drive to top their chosen fields, in turn building the country's production, commerce and, ultimately, the economy.

And all because of *Countdown's* brave decision to hire the all-inspiring Sam Broadley as the new fresh face of Channel 4! Think of the headlines:

COUNTDOWN KOs CREDIT CRUNCH!

My friends at Channel 4... don't find yourselves stuck in a conundrum. Hire me. Mark my words, *Countdown's* number will not be up.

I look forward to hearing from you with regards my application and the very real prospect of working together in the near future, whenever Des's contract is up. Which I hope is soon.

Yours faithfully,

Sam Broadley

Sam Broadley

███████████

███████████

Ipswich

Suffolk

███████

20th September, 2008

Dear Channel 4,

On the back of the disturbing news of Carol Vorderman's imminent departure, I am taking full advantage by writing to formally apply for the position of **Mathematician** of *Countdown*.

Now, if you are following employment regulation and sifting through all applications thoroughly, as I'm sure you are, you will be vigilant enough to notice that only yesterday I applied for **Presenter** of *Countdown*! (Sam Broadley, 27, former (suspected) agoraphobic/ inactive student). I will admit my first choice would be to join the show as Presenter, but if for any (unfathomable) reason I would be deemed unsuitable, I would definitely be equally delighted to man the *Countdown* calculator.

At first, I was hugely upset at Carol's decision to leave the show citing reasons of remuneration. Having been the sweetheart of Channel 4 since its inception, I felt she would go well past retirement age with *Countdown*, but instead, her stockpile of fans have been left devastated by her decision to quit – especially as it was based on the bucks.

But I am not going to sit here and write of my contempt for Carol. How could I? She is an amazing woman who has held a space all of her own in my heart since the moment I clapped eyes on her.

But not based on her looks. Certainly not. Not in the early days, anyway. She is one of the few people on Earth who have actually got better-looking as they have grown older. She has gone from a plain Jane, wouldn't-look-twice youngster to a fine, elegant and beautiful mature woman. I don't know her specific age but she's certainly not too old for me to have a crack. With curves in all the right places, she is one sexy chick! I'd certainly ask Carol for two from the top!

It isn't just her mathematical magic I admire – her dieting methods are profound and have resulted in her developing that body of lustful appeal. I appreciate the scientific demonstration of her weight management through the medium of good food. I have actually dabbled in her detox methods. Whilst at university, I developed some sort of obesity. Clinical apparently, but not necessarily obvious (unless your naked eye happened to be fixed upon my naked body…). Nevertheless, I decided I should make an effort to rid the rolls so set about following in the footsteps of my heroine and wrote a five-week detox plan.

I should admit that I took Wednesdays off the diet because this was football day at university, which was always followed up by a massive drinking binge (alcohol is banned on the diet). In turn, this quite often resulted in writing off Thursdays due to the required grease-ridden recovery food (grease-ridden food being banned on the diet). Sadly, I discovered that actually there was little point in detoxing for just five days per week – less so for even fewer days, which I found out as my motivation simultaneously spiralled.

I remained chubby.

Yes, chubby, but cutely so. Whilst excess fat on some can be truly repulsive, it seems I have been dealt a lucky hand. My portly features are endearing, so my mum tells me. I ask you, please do not assume that my appearance is not suitable for television, or if it *is* suitable, only for widescreen. I am willing to send you a photo for proof upon request. It will also help you to identify me when I arrive for interview.

In terms of my non-shallow credentials to become Mathematician for *Countdown*, I have some. I won't lie and claim to be a maths mastermind, but I am certainly arithmetically able. Not only did I win a Grade C in GCSE Mathematics through hard work and endeavour, I also own a mean scientific calculator! I believe in the shortcuts in life, getting from A to B by the shortest possible route. Why bother trying to work out how to hit 898 with one from the top and five from the bottom when a) that's the contestants' job, and b) a machine can do it for me? I am a logical person. That's not logical.

It's that kind of innovative thinking that gets me places. I suggest you at *Countdown* adopt a similar attitude. Implement new and contemporary thinking processes. Hey, here's an idea: I'll be Presenter AND Mathematician! I just came up with that inspiration as I'm writing. See – always thinking innovatively. Let's face it, neither job is taxing. I could do both jobs with my eyes shut. (If I did do that, you'd have to let me know which numbers came up so I can type them into my now-Braille calculator)

If you were to take me on, I would be happy to not only take the same salary as was on the table for Carol but do both jobs. You can't lose. You get a top-class Presenter and Calculator Operator at only half the cost. If you know your numbers like I do, you'll know that 2-4-1 is the most mathematically sound formula. It's good business sense.

I challenge you, then, *Countdown*, to take the show and Channel

4 into a new era, severing all ties with the old-fashioned, stale, dank history, oozing mustiness. It's time for a fresh face. My plan is to implement a much more youthful look to the show. Out go the 90-somethings in the audience, in comes a new energetic crowd, similar in style to that of *Top of the Pops*.

Let's make Carol suffer inevitable regret at her farcical decision to leave *Countdown* in limbo.

I look forward to hearing from you regarding my application(s).

Yours faithfully,

Sam Broadley

21st October, 2008

Dear Sam,

Thank you for your letter regarding Countdown.

Apologies that it has taken a while to answer your letter, we are currently dealing with large volumes of post and it has taken longer than usual to reply.

We are delighted at your interest wanting to work on the show. We would advise, however, that there is no longer an opportunity to apply for the programme.

The programme-makers did hold an open application to find a replacement for Carol Vorderman, however, the closing date to apply for the position was Friday 19th September, 2008. The programme-makers are currently working their way through the applications received. The new Countdown recruit will be seen on screen for the new series in January, 2009.

In regards to a replacement for Des, the show's producers are doing this via a closed process. They will be choosing a known host to take over from Des.

Thank you again for taking the time to contact us here at Channel 4 and for your interest in our programming.

Kind regards,

Channel 4 Viewer Enquiries

Sam Broadley

██████████████

██████████████

Ipswich

Suffolk

██████████

2nd October, 2008

Dear Mr. Boris Johnson,

'Ello 'ello 'ello!

I am writing to formally apply for the position of **Commissioner** of the Metropolitan Police Force.

As the new Mayor of London (congratulations, by the way), you won't have been shocked by the shock resignation of Sir Ian Blair from his post as Commissioner. Mainly because you encouraged it. I found myself glued to the television all day as respected figures expressed their astonishment at the news. Some were in despair that the poor chap was forced out.

I for one am delighted: a) It gives me the opportunity to apply to become Commissioner, and b) I didn't like the bloke anyway.

I don't think I'm on my own, either. It was clear from the beginning of your tenure that your confidence in Sir Ian was lower than the Devil's cellar. He made errors from the outset. I won't go into any detail but I think we both know he gravely misjudged certain scenarios. Probably the most successful thing the man did was to stay in the job as long as he did!

But while the tabloids and Home Secretary Jacqui Smith dwell, let's not, you and I. It's time to look for the next man to head this great nation's police force, to lead from the front, to finally win the seemingly endless fight against Team Crime.

This is where I, a lovely leader-of-the-line, come in.

Hailing from Suffolk, I am a man with experience. I have recently ceased employment with Norfolk Police. Not as a policeman but as a Crime Investigator. A cool title but not a cool job. I dealt with the sad victims of brutal non-emergency crimes, such as theft of flowers from the gardens of old ladies and the mindless vandalism of trampolines. I later moved into the main control room where I would take the incoming 999 calls, a role in which I could encounter the whole range of scenarios, from child hoax calls to mental patients escaping from the cells with a desire to bite people to knife-wielding estranged wives chasing after their husbands' love-children. It really could be anything.

But it was a challenge I loved. I loved telling the hoax kids that I knew where they were and a police dog was on its way round to rip their lying lips off, for example.

So why did I leave? Excellent question, Boris, really very good. Well, it's quite simple: I couldn't get high enough quickly enough. I am the sort of person that needs complete control very early on. Not because I can't deal with authority or because I have delusions of grandeur. It's because I am aware in my own mind that I have the capacity within my brain to effect positive change upon failing projects. I am the best.

Norfolk is by no means the most dangerous county in the UK. But within the Force, there were a number of fundamental flaws obvious to the naked eye from the day I walked in. I wanted to make changes but had no power or influence to do so.

A question for you, Boris: Why is it called common sense when it's not very common? It's a poser that's stumped me for years.

I find it in all walks of life, bewildering examples of a lack of basic brainpower and logical thinking processes where we end up with staggering results of disaster, tragedy and travesty.

I admire you, Boris. You are a man after my own heart. Yes, you may be some years older, middle-class, very well-spoken, have had decades of experience in politics and wisdom to match, a career in television behind you (and possibly ahead), attractive on the eye with a head of big, blonde hair and have amassed a following of loads of female admirers; and I may be young (27), the less-good kind of middle-class, have had a less-monied upbringing, no experience of politics, a non-respected Suffolk accent, dark-haired (cropped) with no followers of note; but our similarities are endless.

We are both very intelligent people and possess a decent grasp of that little thing 'common sense'. Whilst this is a vital attribute to run a city or police force, it's not the most important. The essential characteristic is… charisma. You and I enjoy an abundance of both.

I think it's obvious that we are the two most charismatic and common-sensical blokes to walk the green and pleasant land. So imagine if we worked together. Just imagine. A handsome match made in beautiful Heaven. Let's put right the wrongs in society and help bring the pride back to our public.

Use that common sense of yours, Boris. Bring me in. Make *me* Top Cop. It will go down as one of your finest political moves of all time.

I look forward to hearing from you very soon, Boris. You can't wait to meet me…

Yours sincerely,

Sam Broadley

GREATER **LONDON** AUTHORITY

Mayor's Office
Greater London Authority

24th November, 2008

Dear Sam Broadley,

Thank you for your correspondence to the Mayor, which has been passed to me for reply. Your letter makes reference to your desire to apply for the role of Commissioner of the Metropolitan Police Service. You will need to apply through the formal channels.

The Home Office and the Metropolitan Police Authority (MPA) are jointly advertising the position. The appointment will be made by Her Majesty The Queen following a recommendation by the Home Secretary under the Police Act 1996.

Before making her recommendation, the Home Secretary will have regard to any recommendations made to her by the MPA and any representations from the Mayor of London. The successful applicant will be appointed in spring 2009 at the latest. The appointment will be for a period of five years.

To apply, please contact:
Victoria ▮▮▮▮▮▮
Home Office
▮▮▮▮▮▮▮▮▮▮
▮▮▮▮▮▮▮
London
▮▮▮▮
Telephone: ▮▮▮▮▮▮
Email: ▮▮▮▮▮▮▮▮▮▮▮▮▮

Thank you again for getting in touch with the Mayor of London on this matter.

Yours sincerely,

Community Safety Team

Sam Broadley

██████████████

██████████████

Ipswich

Suffolk

██████████

1st December, 2008

Dear Ms Victoria ██████████,

I do hope you don't mind me writing to you directly like this, only I was given your name and contact details by the London Mayor, Boris Johnson('s office). It's in connection with the currently available position of **Commissioner** of the Metropolitan Police Force. Now you know that, you'll remember that you are indeed expecting applications for the post and so won't mind me writing to you at all!

Boris('s office) asked me to write to you, Victoria, after I sent him a letter of application. I have made the assumption that I impressed to a suitable degree, hence the reason you are reading this letter. I do very much hope to be successful at this second stage of the recruitment process. I wouldn't half love an interview!

Thinking about it, my letter to Boris was so intriguing, I imagine, that he's probably told you all about me and to expect to receive some excellent correspondence from yours truly. Therefore, there is very little point in me reiterating my previous words so I'm going to write some new ones. By new ones, I don't mean newly-made-up words, you know, that you wouldn't find in the Oxford English Dictionary, like 'asheck' or 'duddo', just existing ones that I didn't use in my letter to Boris so as to keep it fresh. Well, *some* of the words will be the same. Some already have been repeated, like 'the' and 'and'; I've *definitely* used those in both letters. And I suspect there are others. I suppose what I'm trying to say is that I'm going to give you new sentences. By which I mean sentences not utilised in my first-stage application.

I think the best thing I can do is to specify specifically some specifics on how I intend to run the Police Force. And it does needs running. Obviously. By me.

The first thing you will learn about me when we meet at the interview, apart from being incredibly engaging, is that I am such a methodical and radical thinker. By that, I mean I think about things methodically and radically. So in the years I've been building up to this moment of applying, all my thinking has been about methods and radicalness. Let me explain.

I've had to watch in the news for years about where the Force has been going wrong, and being the gifted man I am, I've been able to come up with solutions to a lot of the problems we face in our society. And now, finally, my chance is here to get in and implement my plans to rid London and all cities, towns, boroughs, suburbs, estates, villages, fields and beaches of criminal practices once and for all. Literally, there will be no more crime. What a cool prospect that is!

So what's one of the things that is annoying most people just lately? No, not Katie Price. I mean, yes, she *is* annoying, but I mean in the world of criminality. It's gang culture. And this monstrosity is one of the hundreds of things I have solved (in theory).

What are the reasons youth gangs form? Well, it's fair to say that humans are pack animals. We thrive when we work in teams. Sadly, many of the youngsters of today don't feel they can fit into any particular conventional group. So they form their own, and we call them gangs.

Humans are also territorial. That's why normal people buy or rent houses and then tend to live in them. They lock the doors to keep others out. Windows are commonly installed during the building stage of a house, primarily to keep a look-out for possible trespassers and potential harm-doers. That's the big advantage of living in a high-rise block of flats: you can see for miles if you live in one of the top ones. Unless there's another block of flats right across the road, in which case one might be able to see into other flats' windows, which brings alternative potential benefits…

The point is that gangs live by the same human instincts as the classy folk like you and I, Victoria, just in different ways. (I've made the assumption you're a class act based on your standing in society and the position you hold – I promise I've not pursued or stalked you in any way whatsoever to learn this. I am also sorry if you happen to live on a council estate in a flat that contains windows overlooked by the flats of perverts opposite (I don't live in a flat across from you, nor anywhere else, for that matter).) The first instinct is for them to survive, and part of that is packing together and defending territory. (The second instinct, by the way, is to procreate, hence the upsurge in children having children.)

The trouble with their choice of methods for territory-defending and, indeed, hierarchy-deciding is that they tend to commit a lot of crimes, what with all the violence and theft. *This* is what we need to put a stop to. And *this* is how I'm going to do it:

We're going to hire undercover coplets. Yes – child officers.

This brilliant innovation in the way we police going forward will change the face of gang culture and clean up our youth-ridden streets once and for all. We will hire thousands of kids of all ages, train them up as full police officers, but with the sole aim of sending them out on to the streets to infiltrate the gangs. Each coplet will be given a new identity and a history to match that of your typical thug, things that command instant respect among the gang-types.

Once they are entirely prepared, it is up to them to get out there and make a name for themselves on the streets, win the trust and friendship of the leader of their chosen gang and then live that life. They will observe the gang in action, noting certain behaviours and traits of individuals, plans for attacking rivals, ways in which they intend on bringing down society. Intermittently and in code, they will report their findings back to the seniors in their Force so we can prepare to launch an attack of our own to prevent criminal activities and take out the ringleaders.

Our coplets will be fully-trained in street-fighting and weaponry in preparation for any spontaneous brawls that might occur while they are on duty undercover. Their safety is of paramount importance. Also as part of their training, they will watch those films where cops go undercover to bring down Mafia dons and the like. I know they nearly all have age 18 certificates, but they'll give our kids great ideas and the confidence to head into the warzone knowing they can win, even though it'll mean a life under witness protection for them and their entire families when they finally get found out after dobbing all the baddies in.

In terms of the ages of our coplet intakes, well, it's all about matching up with the gangs. Until recent times, you'd probably think your typical gang was aged in the mid-teenage years. But they're getting younger and younger these days so we will have no choice but to take in equally young recruits to get into these gangs. It's a shame to have to take kids who are in single figures, but if that's what we have to do to clean up this country, then so be it. In fact, I'm hearing bad things about toddlers in nurseries and related gang warfare.

They just grow up so quickly these days. So sad.

It's also vitally important the coplets' parents never find out during their periods of duty undercover. Mums and dads are emotional creatures (you just have to meet mine) and tend to think of their kids' welfare as the single most important thing in the world. Well, I beg to differ. What about the safety of everyone else, huh? Selfish. We can't be hiring these kids with their parents knowing because they'll fear for their children's safety and blow their cover – inadvertently *creating* danger for their little cherubs. That's how stupid parents can be.

So they must not find out. We'll have to concoct stories to feed them for when the coplets are out for nights at a time, like they're off on a week-long school field trip or something. We'll need to create some permission slips for that, thinking about it, and be careful they're not on police-issued headed-paper.

Victoria, I'm not sure if you're the ultimate decision-maker in this process or not. Well, I *know* you're not – that little pleasure goes to Her Majesty The Queen. But whether or not you have an influence in matters of persuading our good lady, you'll surely agree that this idea (remembering that it is one of bloody *loads* I've got) is a winner. I can't believe no-one else has thought of it.

There are just so many benefits. We rid our communities of horrible kids, we make immediate respectable adults of the good kids aged three-up and those kids will happily work undercover for regular bags of sweets, meaning massive savings in wages and adult police officers because we won't need as many thanks to our coplets clearing the streets of scum!

Wow, my mind is blown with excitement. I can tell yours is, too, even though you haven't read this yet in my time. That's how good my anticipation of people's thoughts is.

Victoria, I am so confident in my ability to be the Chief of the Met. I am absolutely the perfect man for the job, what with my existing experience with Norfolk Police and my amazing ideas to revolutionise how we police in London and beyond.

Please ensure you head directly to the Palace and tell the Queen you've got your man. Let's not even bother with the interview.

I look forward to hearing from you very soon. Or The Queen.

Yours sincerely,

Sam Broadley

Sam Broadley

Ipswich
Suffolk

9th December, 2008

To Her Majesty Queen Elizabeth II,

It gives me great pleasure to write to you with regards a recent formal application I made for the position of **Commissioner** of the Metropolitan Police Force.

My initial application was made to London Mayor Boris Johnson by written letter. Via a colleague, he wrote back encouraging me to further write to the Home Office as the next stage of my application. Mr. Johnson informed me that the Monarch ultimately makes the decision of who to appoint as Commissioner, albeit on the recommendation of the Home Secretary.

I have completed the second part of my application but I thought it would be a good idea to make early contact with you, Your Majesty, as I hope one day soon to be meeting you face-to-face over tea at the Palace to discuss how I intend on taking the Police Force forward.

I had to think long and hard as to whether I should put this letter together for you, Your Royalness, for I know you are, as our Monarch, a busy lady and have many appointments and duties to tend to. In fact, I have taken it upon myself to look at your forthcoming diary commitments. (Not your private diary/memoirs; I have no access, and even if I did, I would resist all temptation to take a peek because

I respect people's privacy, unless they are criminals, in which case they don't deserve my respect and I would take any opportunity to read their diaries; aside from the entertainment value, it might actually reveal some damning evidence. That's the cop in me – always on the lookout...)

I noticed from your diary that you have several forthcoming appointments. I was very surprised, actually, to see you're working on Christmas Day! It says that you will be giving a speech to the people of our Great Britain, discussing the highs and lows of the past year and the challenges ahead for 2009. I would've thought the Queen of England would be allowed to have Christmas Day off. In fact, I am sure you are permitted to take it as holiday, but what makes you a very special lady, Your Highness, is that you are not too big even as Queen to be doing an honest day's work, even on this the world-recognised ultimate holiday day, if it means raising the spirits of the people you reign over. Good on you. I bet the King of America wouldn't do that.

As for my application to become Commissioner, I do not wish to turn this letter into an attempt to sell myself to you, Your Worship. I feel I am doing that quite successfully through the conventional channels. My sole objective here is to make an introduction to you, to begin our acquaintance early on. I say acquaintance; that's a term I associate with two or more people who are involved in a formal relationship, usually within a working environment. I expect our relationship to begin as a formal one, but I like to think that as time goes on and we become better acquainted, we can become genuine friends.

To be Commissioner is tough with so many challenges, but challenges are what I thrive on and I will work long, long hours to hit my personals targets of change. As time goes by and you see how successful I become, I will earn your respect. You will also see my natural charisma shine through – it's one of my biggest attributes. I'm fun to be around and I think you'll want to not only work alongside me but spend some time with me on a social level. Perhaps, as I settle into the job, we could mix business with pleasure and hit some wine bars when I finish the odd long shift where we can talk about my progress and you can help me unwind.

Eventually, I would like to meet some of your family. Your husband HRH Prince Philip is a personal favourite. I have never met him so I can only judge by his media appearances, but I like what I see and read. It's so easy for a Royal to sit back and remain formal throughout his/her life and play the role of a robot. People forget that even Royals are human with personalities and characteristics. Bravo to the Prince for becoming the one to offer himself as a regular bloke with charisma and humour.

This is not to put you down, Your Majesty. While it comes naturally to Philip to present his true relaxed self to the world, I know you find it a little bit more difficult. That's understandable considering your job is the most famous in the world and you are under a brighter spotlight. But I am an excellent judge of character (you have to be as Commissioner). I can spot the real person in their eyes. You have all it takes to be a highly entertaining lady in a whole new way than we are used to seeing. If you hadn't been born a Royal, I'm confident you would have had a career on stage or in the circus. Of that I have no doubt. And it's this character which makes me excited about chilling with you and putting the world to rights over a glass or two of wine.

You will have heard, I am sure, of your namesake Queen, the rock band. Through the medium of music, they had a mammoth influence on the lives of tens of millions of people around the world over two decades, nearly all of it good, and will continue to do so. I am not exaggerating when I say you have done the same but tenfold and for some thirty years longer. I take great strength from having watched you over the years, Ma'am. You are my heroine and my true influence in life. I want to do the same for you as you have done for me.

Your Highness, I so hope to pass the rigours of the application process to become Commissioner. I love this country and wish to serve your people – our people – to the best of my ability and beyond. This job is the world and more to me and I hope I can count on your, what is ultimately the winning, vote.

I very much look forward to receiving a written reply from you, my Queen, and meeting with you soon on a formal basis with a view to serving you and winning your lifelong friendship.

Yours sincerely,

Sam Broadley

BUCKINGHAM PALACE

16th January, 2009

Dear Mr. Broadley,

The Queen has asked me to thank you for your letter of 9th December, and to say that Her Majesty has taken careful note of the views you express regarding your recent application for the post of Metropolitan Police Commissioner.

Your thoughtfulness in writing as you did is appreciated.

Yours sincerely,

Correspondence Officer

Sam Broadley, Esq.

Sam Broadley

██████████

██████████

Ipswich

Suffolk

██████████

30th December, 2008

Dear Mr. Ed Balls,

I am writing to formally apply for the currently available position of **Chief of Exams** for the Government's watchdog, The Qualifications & Curriculums Authority.

You will be well aware as Secretary for Schools of the furore of this year's SATs tests for 11-to-14-year-olds. To remind you in case you have forgotten, of the 1.2 million children who took the exams, up to 100,000 received their results late, and several *never did*. The then-Chief of Exams, Dr. Ken Boston, resigned (jumped before shoved) having predicted a damning report on the fiasco. What a great prediction. If only he had had such foresight before the exams debacle, maybe he could have prevented it, saved his job and retained his self-respect.

But he didn't. A farce was born. It could so easily have been avoided but wasn't. That is the surest sign possible that it is time for not only change but a complete overhaul.

This is where I, an extrovert examiner of examinations, come in.

Not by trade, of course. But I can tell you that it's been a personal quest to consistently analyse the use and effectiveness of exams ever since I began taking such tests back in my early school years. I have felt a strong desire to know the value of a child being assessed under virtual military conditions to see if they've learnt stuff or not. This thirst for knowledge has driven me to make it my business to unofficially watch out for the comings and goings of examinational processes and their outcomes.

My conclusion: I'm not happy. Like you, I was unimpressed by the QCA and their inability to do the one thing asked of them and step in when things were going nipples up. It was clearly time for Boston to do one. Now, having completed the unofficial role I gave myself of monitoring the education game, and examinations in particular, I feel my time has come to persuade you, Mr. Balls, that I am the man to take full control of the red pen during these testing times and convince you that my school of thought is the correct one.

But why should I be given a role with the power to influence the education of millions of children across England and Wales? Well, if I'm honest, I did question my suitability for the job, not based on my knowledge of the subject, which I consider to be vast, but I was unsure as to the formal qualifications required for the job. But after some thinking, I realised there are obviously no direct prerequisites or particular certificates required, as demonstrated by Dr. Ken Boston. In fact, the more I thought about it, the more I was surprised that a *doctor* was head of an exams watchdog. I would have thought his duties surely laid in diagnosing illnesses or performing surgery, not in checking on examiners.

Then I suddenly realised why he was hired for Head of Exams: because becoming a doctor requires taking and passing more exams than any other profession. They study for years and years, their work constantly scrutinised and tested to prove they are capable of looking after the health of people and some animals. Therefore, who is more qualified to become Head of Exams than Doctor Boston who has had more tests than a new perfume?!

Of course, you will know what I mean through your own experiences. I am aware that you are very well-educated in the field of economics, and indeed you were expected to walk into the role of Chancellor when Mr. Brown stepped up to Boss, but you ended up as Secretary for Schools. My guess is that Gordon, being the obviously charismatic and funny man he is, chose you for the role based on the Cockney rhyming slang – Ed Balls: Schools!

But I am perfect for the role of Chief of Exams because I have *taken* exams. Admittedly not as many as a doctor but several nonetheless. A good fifteen or so. I know what it's like to go through the strains of revision, pre-exam cramming, the anxious weeks of waiting for the results knowing that one's life can be made or broken by one letter on a scrap of paper.

It is the years of suffering I went through to gain my excellent grades back in the late '90s (including a superb A* in GCSE PE (don't be fooled by the physical nature of this subject; it was way more academically difficult than you'd think)) that have made me decide on a testing revamp once I take the top seat. Through talks with you, Mr. Balls, I will be making many changes to give our children the best chance of succeeding in education.

I will let you know early (now) that I will in fact be scrapping *all* examinations as we know them. Instead, testing of pupils' knowledge shall be taking place through the one format that brings the nation together: gameshows. It is something that I have thought long and hard about and I have penned a detailed plan which I would be delighted to take you through during my interview.

Popular family shows such as *Who Wants to Be a Millionaire?*, *Weakest Link* and *Countdown* will be transformed to take the shape of our children's GCSE exams. In place of the examinations for high-level qualifications, such as lawyers, politicians and architects, tougher formats will be employed, such as *Mastermind, University Challenge* (apt) and *Eggheads*. Other shows currently under consideration include *Deal Or No Deal, Blockbusters* and *Going For Gold.*

For me, Ed, it's important to take the pressure off the kids during what are clearly stressful times. What better way to do this than take the gameshow format which everyone enjoys whilst retaining a serious and vital examination process in which everyone who succeeds will have something to offer society.

Schools are currently in disarray and this latest exams fiasco is doing nothing for Labour's reputation. Let me help you. Let me apply my format to allow pupils and students to use their buzzers and voices in front of studio audiences to prove their knowledge and worthiness to earn grades and qualifications. One chat with me and you'll agree this is the only way forward.

I look forward to speaking with you soon and working together to make our lacking children great for once.

Yours sincerely,

Sam Broadley

department for
children, schools and families

6th February, 2009

Dear Sam,

Thank you for your letter of 30th December, 2008 to the Rt. Hon. Ed Balls MP in connection with the position of Chief Executive of the Qualifications and Curriculum Authority (QCA). Your letter has been passed to me for a reply as I work within the QCA, Ofqual and Examinations Delivery Division.

It may be helpful if I begin by explaining the current position with regard to the post of Chief Executive of QCA. Although Dr. Ken Boston offered his resignation just before the publication of a report into the delivery of the 2008 National Curriculum Tests, the board of QCA has decided to consider the report more fully before taking a view on whether to accept his resignation. As a result, Dr. Boston is currently suspended from his post until that review is concluded. In the interim, Andrew Hall, QCA's Director Strategic Resource Management, has been appointed Acting Chief Executive.

Should a formal appointments process begin in due course, the details of the qualities and experience required for the post, along with the application process, will be made publicly available.

For further information regarding the work of QCA, and the report into the delivery of the National Curriculum Tests for 2008, please visit their website at: www.qca.org.uk.

Yours sincerely,

QCA, Ofqual and Examinations Delivery Division

Sam Broadley

█████████████
█████████████

Ipswich
Suffolk

███████████

7th January, 2009

Dear Mr. Giles Clarke,

I am writing to formally apply for the currently available position of **England Cricket Captain**.

As Chairman of the England and Wales Cricket Board, you will not be relishing the task of selecting yet another captain so soon after making what seemed to be the ideal decision back in the summer of '08. Despite the brilliant Pietersen effectively being a foreigner (I say effectively, I mean unequivocally), his talent as a batsman, his infectious charisma and his obvious patriotism for his newly-found home country made him the perfect choice.

Or so it seemed. It's quite simple: you cannot have two gigantic egos pulling in different directions in one team. We will not find elusive success like that. Kevin, despite his talents, clearly could not accept that Moores is a quality cricket coach who is capable of reaching the heady heights of some victories given time. Yes, he has led no notable victories to date; no, he is not highly regarded by senior members of the England team and English cricket in general; yes, he lacks the good looks and sexy wife possessed by Kevin; but that does not mean he will not deliver success one day. Kevin needed to realise that.

You will not find a bigger fan of Kevin Peter Pietersen than me. He is the man that rekindled my love affair with the game of cricket several years ago (three) with his inspiring performances against that arch enemy. No, not Germany, not Scotland, but Australia. The country who, much like America in their own way, revel in their arrogance over their own success, taunt the English because of our sporting failures and mishaps, mouth off in the build-up to clashes between the countries – all this despite the fact they're essentially English! Not just any English but criminal ones! (Please do not make this letter public upon my employment for I do not wish to be sued for libel – it would harm us both. Not that they'd have much of a case – it is a fact after all. Well, maybe not all *current* Australians, that is, ones that are alive today, but *all* of their earliest Oz-dwelling ancestors *definitely* were, and they will *definitely* have passed down those criminal-thinking genes.)

As a direct result of both hiring and firing Pietersen within a matter a months, it is time for you and your board, Clarkey, to have a serious rethink about where the England cricket team is going and who really is best to head it.

This is where I, a cracking cricketer with incredible captaincy qualities, come in.

The last time this job become vacant back in August '08, I didn't get to apply because of your swift decision to hire the beautiful Pietersen. I was disappointed to miss out on at least being heard, but I was satisfied with your choice. Wrongly, as it was proved. This time, I have no intentions of being overlooked, for the good of English and world cricket.

At 28 years of age, I am in prime condition to hit the top of cricket. My guess is that you have not heard of Sam Douglas Broadley, the reason being that I do not currently play first-class cricket. But do not let that put you off; I am still a first-class cricketer. I just need to start playing again.

It's a regret of mine to not have pursued a career in cricket, such were my talents growing up. It started when my dad (not a cricketing man) taught me the wonderful game of French cricket when I was six. The game required huge amounts of skill and concentration – especially as my dad insisted on playing with a real cricket ball! My poor bloody shins! (I'm pretty sure pads hadn't been invented back then.)

My love for bat and ball soon became obvious. Later, having developed a distaste for all things French, I moved into proper cricket aged ten. Soon, I was touted for big things on the cricket pitch. People expected me to become the next Graham Gooch. But my hero was "Beefy" Ian Botham. Not only was he a world-class batter and bowler like me, he loved football and played professionally so. Just like I should have.

My equal love during my childhood was football, and I excelled. Despite my arguments that I was just like Beefy and could do both, I was told to choose. To my regret, I chose football. I'm ashamed to say it was down to money. I wasn't offered any at the time for either sport but I thought I might earn loads in the future playing soccer. I was dreadfully wrong.

Not a day goes by when I don't regret that decision aged just 14. But my new year's resolution, Mr. Clarke, is to look only forward in life, to affect my future course of destiny. I want nothing more than to be a national hero – and I will be thanks to you.

Giles, think not of the controversy, the national uproar, the longevity of a tabloid-led hate campaign against such a seemingly outrageous decision to draft in a total unknown straight to the Captain's chair. Remember why you got into the job in the first place: to bring success.

I cannot wait to lead my team against Australia for the Ashes. That is where the baying crowds, thirsty for my blood, will warm to me, love me and want to have my babies.

I won't bail; I will sweep us to success. I see no boundary to our accomplishments. I will not be stumped. Defeats I will spin into wins. We'll bowl them over, you'll see. When you witness the magnitude of the victory, how devastatingly crushed the Aussies will be, you'll be creasing up with laughter!

I look forward to meeting with you very soon, Mr. Clarke, when I will field your questions. You will like me very much.

Yours sincerely,

Sam Broadley

Sam Broadley

███████████

███████████

Ipswich

Suffolk

███████

15th February, 2009

Dear Professor Stephen Hawking,

I am writing to formally apply for the position of **Lucasian Professor of Mathematics** at Cambridge University.

I must say that I was initially perplexed when I heard your announcement during an interview on *The One Show* that you are due to retire from the world's most celebrated academic chair. Why would someone like yourself want to give up such a prestigious position that you've held for the best part of 30 (29) years? And then I realised that must be the very reason: (nearly) three decades is a long time to stay in any job, let alone one of such pressure to find tough stuff out.

So it's time for you to vacate the most famous seat, second only to the throne of the Queen. It's a role which is key to mankind's development in all things mathematical and astronomical, so it's obvious to all that it's imperative the next person to become Top Prof. must absolutely have the braininess to step into your boots and continue your innovative work and thinking processes. He must change the world.

This is where I, the people's professor, come in.

As a 28-year-old graduate of GCSE Mathematics and Co-ordinated Science (covering the disciplines of Chemistry, Biology and Physics),

I'm the man to take the reins. I've always had a fascination, an enthralment, with the workings of the world and universe. There are questions I need answers to and it has become an obsession to strive for them. I *will* find them, be assured.

Your sole quest, Stephen, is to find out how the universe and everything in it works. That is what you want to know before you leave this life. Whilst a commendable ambition, my mission goes further than just how it all works – I want to know *if, what* and *why.* You get me?

My questions are age-old and childish. Why does the universe exist? If it began with a big explosion, what did it explode into? What is beyond the universe? Is it Dreamland (my own theory)? Is there a god? If so, did he create the Big Bang? If so, was it Dreamland in which he lived? Who gave birth to God? Is there a Mrs. God? Is there actually a brain, that of God or someone/something else behind the creation of Earth and Sun or do we exist through a random sequence of naturally-occurring events? What is the point of it all? Is time-travel actually possible? If so, who among us are from the future and are they fleecing the bookies because they know the horseracing results? Is Elvis really dead? Must we have spiders?

I cannot and will not rest until I have the answers to all these questions and more. If it takes me the rest of my life to know, I'll do it. If I have to create a drug for everlasting life, I'll do it.

You and I are similar in many of our traits, Stephen. We are inquisitive people. Despite our significantly advanced brainpower and knowledge beyond the realms of Average Joe's comprehension, we are in the business of learning. People assume the likes of us know everything, but we don't. We bloody will, though.

While everyone asks questions like the ones I pose, that's all they are to them: questions. To you and I, they are challenges. We have a thirst to discover things previously unbeknown to any man of our age or any other (by 'age', I mean in terms of generations of human life, not our respective accumulated years as individual living beings, although that would be covered by my point also).

To find the answers, we need to flex our mathematical muscles to degrees never before known. Simple sums won't do. We're talking combinations of numbers and formulas one could never imagine originating. The basics of trigonometry and equations belong to the past, for I will be applying a form of mathematics never before seen by man – it shall be known as Magic Maths.

You've not heard of Magic Maths but it will be revolutionary. Too complex to put to you in a little letter, but you should be excited, even now. It's in the early stages of development, but it will change life as we know it. It really is awesome, an American adjective I am loathed to utilise such is my distaste for Americanisms – I'm English, after all, and they have littered our language with their word-dumps. That's not me criticising your incredible voice-technology and its American accent. You have the freedom to use it as you wish. I'm just saying that I don't like what they have done to our language. And in any case, your accent is American but you still use the language as an Englishman, and I thank you for that.

But the point is that Magic Maths will answer questions previously thought impossible to answer, and that's why it's magic. I predict that it will ultimately tell us of the existence or not of God Him(or Her)self.

I believe God to be a chap, and when I do discover God, and possibly Mrs. God, it will go down as the biggest hide-and-seek victory ever seen in the history of the game. I think He/She will be very proud of Professor Sam Douglas Broadley for such a victory.

I'm thinking ahead, of course, maybe several months or even years. But it's my target. As for my application, I hope to have excited you with my future endeavours, but I am not aware of who is on the selection panel or if you are part of it. Maybe you have no say whatsoever, maybe you can make recommendations to the actual panel or maybe you *are* the panel. Whatever the case, work your own magic, Stephen, and get me in for a chat if you want the potential to have your dreams realised. I'm the man to make them come true.

I am aware, as you will be, that you were born on 8th January, 1942. You will also be aware, as I am, that a certain Galileo died on that date 300 years previous. A remarkable coincidence or a cheeky divine act to link two brilliant minds by round mathematics? I'll let you know when I've completed my experiments. But here's something to think about when considering me: 8th January, 1642 – Galileo's death; 8th January, 1942 – your birth; 22nd December, 1980 – my birth… See the link?? Brilliant, isn't it?!

The elite list of previous Lucasian Professors over the last few hundred years is an impressive one. Add Broadley to Hawking and Darwin and you've just raised the bar once more. It'll probably never get any higher.

I wait in anticipation of your reply to my application informing me of how I can further improve my chances of becoming the world's top prof.

Yours sincerely,

Professor Sam Broadley

Sam Broadley

Ipswich
Suffolk

3rd June, 2009

Dear Rt. Hon. Mr. Gordon Brown PM,

I am writing to formally apply for the position of **Speaker of the House of Commons**.

Let's get straight to it: politics is in the Brown stuff. All thanks to the expenses scandal, the whole country is raging like a tied-up tiger being tickled on the toes. Political kingpins have toppled like tenpins after 'fessing up to 'legal errors'. Party leaders, like yourself (of Labour), are under tremendous pressure to rid more members of their own teams, to even prosecute and slaughter. The people want blood – and gallons of it.

And in the latest twist to this extraordinary chain of events, the Speaker's gone! The ultimate scapegoat in what would be, if it wasn't such a tragedy, a classic comedy. Poor old Michael Martin. In my eyes, all the politicians who were caught with their fingers in the people's purse and found themselves crushing under the weight of a nation's pressure made a desperate attempt to deflect the attention elsewhere and so pounced upon some weak words spoken by the Speaker.

Horrific, yes, but The House of Commons is in dire need of a real turnaround. It's crying out for a true personality in the high chair to oversee the BCC battles (Brown, Cameron and Clegg).

This is where I, an astounding speaker of the spoken word, come in.

It's true: when it comes to speaking, I am excellent. Surely a prerequisite for the job of Speaker. Communicating using the thrilling teamwork of a quick-thinking mind and the concurring sounds created by the brilliant voice box within my throat is what I thrive on. Couple this with outstanding associated facial expressions and you've got your perfect man.

But don't take my word for it, Mr. Brown. Please peruse the following testaments:

"My goodness, Sam, the words that emanate from your mouth really are both wise and witty." BS, Birmingham.

"You know, I really think you should be in the public eye, Sam, so huge numbers can appreciate and enjoy your speaking talents." BS, Bolton.

"Oh, Sammy, how your words inspire me so. Please keep talking. I think I love you." BS, Boston.

Impressive accounts, I think you'll agree. But it's not enough on its own for the job of Speaker. Mental strength, character and knowledge of political proceedings are all essential requirements. Well you're in luck, Gordy, for I possess them all. In abundance.

To give you a related example of real-life experience I have had, my life as a football referee would be the most appropriate. Aged just 16, I began taking charge of matches between teams of Under-7s. This was a totally new environment for me. It was tough to go straight from the comfort of school into such a volatile arena of horrible, tempestuous tinies and in full view of parents baying for blood, believing their little angels were the greatest and could do no wrong, only for me to step in and blow my whistle for a footballing crime. I became a target.

But I found true grit and determination to prove to people I was the right man to lead a football match. I successfully commanded the respect of spectators over a period of weeks in charge, to the point where I was told that I was the greatest leader of people they had ever known.

This has given me great confidence in all areas of my life. I find myself using my strengths as a football referee off the field as well as on it. If I see a heated argument ensuing, whether it be between family members, work colleagues, animals or even strangers in the street, I seem to instinctively blow my whistle (which I carry with me always) and jump in between the couple, group or pack to split them up. I then use my powers of control to sit them down to discuss the issue calmly and resolve appropriately. So far, I have had a success rate of above 98.7%.

Prime Minister Brown, thanks to my sublime knowledge of political proceedings, I am aware there is a course of action the House of Commons must follow before I can be instated as Speaker. I know that at least sixteen politicians must recommend me, and then it would go down to a general vote where I would need a minimum of a 50% backing. I consider myself to be ready to take the seat barring just one problem: I don't even know one politician, let alone sixteen.

I'm asking you, Sir, to invite me to lunch at Parliament and introduce me to some of your colleagues. At least fifteen of them. I don't care who they are. Let me prove to you and them that I have some truly terrific speaking tendencies and I can influence people within seconds. Then I guarantee I will become, at just 28, the youngest-ever elected Speaker of the House of Commons.

I shall be known across the media as:

The Broadley Baby in the High Chair.

I look to forward to meeting with you and umpiring some intriguing political encounters.

Yours sincerely,

Sam Broadley

PS: I promise I'll even let you win all the fights! Sshhh!

10 DOWNING STREET
LONDON SW1A 2AA
www.number10.gov.uk

13th July, 2009

Dear Mr. Broadley,

The Prime Minister has asked me to thank you for your recent letter.

The position of Speaker of the House of Commons is a matter for the Houses of Parliament, therefore this office cannot comment in this issue. I regret that this is not a matter with which Mr. Brown can help you.

Yours sincerely,

████████████

Sam Broadley

██████████████
██████████████

Ipswich
Suffolk
ENGLAND
███████████

15th August, 2009

Dear Mr. Domenicali,

Ciao! (I always thought that meant 'Goodbye', but Google tells me it's 'Hello' as well. I can very much confirm I am saying "Hello!")

Anyway, I am writing to formally apply for the currently available position of **Racing Driver** for your Formula One Ferrari team for the remainder of this season.

It was a double-blow for Ferrari what with Felipe Massa's horrific head injury and subsequent inability to race for the coming weeks and then to be teased by the possible return of the legendary and much-loved Michael Schumacher, only for him to walk away from the challenge citing a neck injury. The whole furore has left Ferrari up the track without a throttle.

With the next race only two weeks away, you will be frantically working out a way of drafting in a super racing driver who can see you through these tough weeks while you wait for Massa to, quite literally, get his head together. You will be looking, no doubt, within your current team of test drivers for a man with the skill and bravery to take the wheel and steer Ferrari to victory.

They say the answers to the tough questions are usually right under your nose. Well, not for this question it isn't. The answer's here in

England. He's writing this letter. Yes, me, Sam Douglas Broadley, or, as I'm widely known on the go-kart circuit, Speedy Sammy Bee (Bee being a play on words of sorts, in that my surname begins with the letter 'B' and I am like a bumble bee in that I am roundly-shaped and it defies science that I am able to fly (as in drive a car) at all, let alone at such incredible speeds with such rotundness).

It's likely you've not heard of me, what with the concerns of your Formula One commitments, but I am an up-and-coming talent. An all-round sportsman, my biggest attribute is my will to win and win big. I have always accepted nothing but the best performances of myself in every sporting activity I have partaken in. I strive to win at all costs. Stick me in a racing car and you'll see just what I'm willing to do. (To give you a clue, I don't mind carrying a few drawing pins to occasionally drop behind me to see off a driver daring to attack my rear.)

Somewhat illogically, my sporting superiority hasn't always panned out in my favour. In fact, I am not a professional sportsman in any capacity so you could say it's *never* panned out in my favour. But that's OK because I love, as everyone does, the story of the underdog rising to the top from nowhere to become world champion.

I'm no spring chicken. At 28, most would say all sporting opportunities are languishing deep within my archives, lying dormant in history forever. Not me, however. I've always believed that there's one more big chance waiting for me. And my belief is that the golden chance has finally arrived courtesy of you, Mr. D. I intend to bring such greatness to the track, such unbelievable speed and flair, that the whole world of people will turn their heads as one in awe of this new superstar, so much so that you won't want Massa back! I mean, you'll want him to get better, obviously, but he won't be welcome back in the car.

I will be the Rocky Balboa of Formula One racing... but cooler and better-looking. And I can speak clearly.

At this point, I want to tell you a bit about my experiences as a driver to help you better understand what I can give to you and your team. This is your chance to get excited about my offerings for Ferrari and this season's campaign to win the Championship.

First off, here's the amusingly ironic part: I don't have a driving licence! It is something to smile about because, on the face of it, how can a non-driver be not only a Formula One racing driver but a challenger for the title as well? Don't dismiss me before I've even left the grid, for I have the formula for success.

I am in the process of learning to drive. In fact, I am close to being test-ready. But throughout the painstaking process of becoming educated on the workings of a motor vehicle and suitably skilled in operating the machine on the mad British roads, my biggest problem has been my speed. Unlike most learner drivers who drive like wary snails, I move with the swiftness of a cheetah. My instructor just cannot hold me back, despite having his own brake pedal!!!

It's like my life as a whole: I'm trying to get somewhere quickly and by the fastest possible route. The speed issue is one I'm trying to control, but recently I have thought: *Why should I?* This is how I'm made. I was born to speed. You don't stop a dog from barking or a bird from flying. Why stop a natural-born speeder from burning up the roads? (I'm not including idiots in this; I'm not an idiot.) It was at this moment of realisation that I knew racing is in my blood.

In the years I have spent not driving cars, I was preparing myself for this day where I could potentially join Formula One competition. First, it was all about *Mario Kart*. I sat on my sofa day after day, week after week, year after year, perfecting every performance on every track, dominating every other character (I played as Mario, the main man (it just seemed fitting)); whether it be Yoshi or Princess, (not sure why a woman was allowed to compete), Mushroom or Toad, or even the big boys of Bowser and Kong, I eventually ruled the virtual karting world.

And so it was finally time to move on to the real thing. And the years of settee-training paid off as I proved to be a truly remarkable driver under real race conditions on both the indoor and outdoor go-karting circuits. I am exceptionally gifted. I've sometimes had to learn the hard way, like the time I wrote off a kart by thinking I could negotiate the hairpin at top speed without brakes. But hey, I'm sure Da Vinci spilt some paint before creating the Mona Lisa.

Britain has created some truly world-class champions over the years, heroes like Stirling Moss, Nigel Mansell and Lewis Hamilton. This year looks set for Jenson Button to take the world stage and steer his way to glory. I don't want that to happen. You don't want that to happen. Together we can make sure it doesn't happen. But only if you get me in immediately. I need a good week to practice in your car because I've never driven such a beast before.

Let me take to the wheel and show you how to really drive a car. I'm different to the rest. I'm a quirky driver. I have a knack for outstanding use of the kerbs, as my driving instructor can verify. Above all, I have the winning mentality. After years of only achieving levels unworthy, I am bursting with energy and literal drive to succeed on the world stage.

Sir, I may never have been to watch a Formula One race live. I may not have a driving licence. I may never have sat behind the wheel of a Formula One racing car. We may be halfway through the season already. I may currently be sitting on zero points in the Drivers' Championship. But one thing is utterly certain: I can win Ferrari the World Championship of 2009.

Meet me. Watch me. Sign me. I'm yours. So is the trophy.

Yours sincerely,

Sam Broadley

PS: By the way, I'd love to start a campaign to get the usage of mushrooms, shells and banana skins in F1 racing. I have that aspect of competition absolutely nailed, so if there is any slight hint of doubt still lingering for you about me, even after I win this year's championship, that would eliminate it entirely! It would also mean I don't have to resort to drawing pins anymore…

Sam Broadley

██████████████

██████████████

Ipswich

Suffolk

████████████

24th October, 2009

Dear Mr. Stuart Rose,

I am writing to formally apply for the currently available position of **Chief Executive** of Marks & Spencer.

As one of the oldest traditional stores of this our Great Britain, M&S holds a special place in the heart of many a person across the country. They were once seen as the biggest and the best, but sadly, monsters have entered the market – namely the supermarkets of Tesco, Sainsbury's and Asda.

Whilst the modern-day competition is seen as very much a good thing with each shop fighting for the biggest slice of the pie, I for one despise it. If we were a competitive country, we'd have won more World Cups. But we haven't. We are a laid-back people and we love nothing more than humble traditions. That is why the nation wept uncontrollably at the sudden collapse of Woolworths, the store adored by millions from north to south and east to west (although I can't help but think we were swimming in rivers of crocodile tears as it was the British public who refused to shop there anymore, thus the thundering fall of the giant).

It is common knowledge that you are to vacate your current post of Chief Executive, staying on as Chairman until 2011. You will leave behind a beautiful company but one which needs to act quickly to avoid plummeting, just like Woollies, into the depths of Hell. I suspect you need someone with outstanding knowledge of the market, of food, of drink, of clothes, of flowers, of staff, of customers, of Christmas and all related presents and, above all, a man who possesses that flair and creativity to take Marks & Spencer to the next level, to become the superpower once more.

This is where I, a supermarket super-maverick, come in.

It's obvious Tesco is number one. They are crushing any competitor who dares stand in their way. Their vision is clear to the trained marketing eye: bit by bit, they are taking over the world. With permission granted, Sir, I want to stop that happening. I am, I believe, the only man in the country – no, the world – who can stop it happening. How? It's time for me to combat the Clubcard…

The Clubcard is the clear leader of all the loyalty schemes available. They've proved to have the suckers rushing to the stores because of the, on the face of it, fabulous Clubcard deals. You'll know, as do I, that Tesco aren't giving anything away. They're making their money somehow – we just don't know how. My personal opinion is that they put some kind of airborne drug into the freshly-baked bread. It's the first thing you smell as you walk in. I must confess that I have found myself wandering the aisles, selecting items involuntarily and at random, having first smelt the wonderful bread-related aromas during several ill-fated trips to my local store.

The very fact they were able to hook someone as strong-willed as myself goes to show we at M&S need to up our game. Let's not roll over and have our bellies tickled. Instead, let's stand our ground, get our hackles up and growl, growl like mad, before launching a vicious offensive against the evils of Tesco. Let's bring on the might of the &More card.

The &More loyalty card needs a serious boost to get it going. It's light years behind the Clubcard. Most would suggest building it bit by bit, planning a long-term campaign to catch the Clubcard up. I disagree with such fools wholeheartedly. We want the lion's share of the market as soon as is physically possible. But how can I do this as Chief Executive? What is my plan? It's quite simple:

Marks & Spencer will enter the space race.

The race is on between the superpower countries around the world to create the first expedition to Mars. Britain, America, Russia, even India. The big guns are battling it out to be the lead nation in the pursuit of intergalactic supremacy.

What an outstanding campaign it would be for M&S to enter the contest. It seems outrageous but think of it. While we run an excellent shop day-to-day, still marketing ourselves as a fabulous store with outstanding quality and value for money, the cream at the top of the tree, meanwhile, ie: you and I, are planning the ultimate commercial campaign.

My vision is that we invest heavily in the space race, hiring the best dozen rocket scientists in the world, poaching staff from rival projects if necessary, and build the biggest, best, fastest and most innovative spaceship ever created.

When the planning stage is complete and the practical process is underway, we go to the press. I'm thinking something along the lines of you and I dressing up as aliens and performing a parachute jump from the edge of space, dropping right into one of our key stores in London during peak shopping hours.

This massive project and publicity stunt will get the country going wild! The people will fall in love with us again – especially with the implementation of the next stage of my plan: collect enough &More points and you will be on the maiden voyage to Mars. That'll get people shopping!

I want you to read this letter again and again to take in the magnitude of what I am saying. You are a sensible man. In time, probably by the end of the day as you read this, you will realise that this is the only way to beat the Tesco demon.

Let Tesco rule the world. Marks & Spencer shall rule the universe.

As my reward for the project's inception, I expect to known as:

Sir Sam Douglas Broadley: Lord of the Galaxy.

I look forward to meeting with you as a priority with a view to entering the finest period in the proud history of Marks & Spencer. I'll be your brightest star, you'll see.

Yours sincerely,

Sam Broadley

Sam Broadley

Ipswich
Suffolk

24th October, 2009

Dear Ms. Sarah Lambert,

I am writing to formally apply for the position of **President** of the European Union.

My letter is to you, Ms Lambert, as the Acting Head of the European Commission Representation in the UK, in the hope that you can get my chronically important message to each of the 27 member-countries across the EU as a priority. As of January 1st, 2010, the role of President, as you are likely aware, is to change from its current format of a six-monthly rolling contract, whereby ownership of the position changes from country to country, to a fixed three-year term for one person with no ties to a current government within the EU.

It has been all across the news over recent weeks that former Prime Minister Tony Blair has made himself available for selection. He is, of course, well-respected across Europe, and indeed the globe, among the elite-types. Coupled with this is his current holding of Peace Negotiator in the Middle East (which, to some, is ironic considering his war-starting antics), showing him off as a good man. These facts seemingly make him the ideal candidate to lead Europe.

But the people would disagree. I think you know, as I do, Sarah, that Mr. Blair is not a popular man among the masses. Currently, he does not hold a place in the British public eye, but his legacy lingers, much like the smell of a torched sewer or the trail of a dirty slug.

I for one like him. I think he did a splendid job as Prime Minister and continues to do so in his new role. But it's the view of the man on the street that counts, not the well-to-do and the elite. And it's the common man, woman and child whom I care about most.

With this in mind, it's time to put up a serious rival to compete against Mr. Blair, one who can take him on head-to-head, to challenge him to the ultimate battle of wits, a fight to the bitter end. Only then will the elite realise that Blair is a job-hopper and a power-mad maniac searching for one more night of glory. It's time for someone with the courage and bravery to step up to the plate and take on this bedevilled crazy-head (allegedly – phew, glad I got that word in there, just in case this letter gets leaked into the public domain; I don't fancy being sued with all his Hellish might!).

This is where I, a stalwart European kingpin, come in.

I have thought long and hard about applying for this position over recent months, the cracks of self-doubt appearing in my armour because of the potential lack of awareness of my beautiful name throughout the member-states of the European Union. Is this a factor that would condemn my application as a running joke at EU meetings where valuable time that should be spent talking about employment, trade and human rights is actually being wasted ridiculing me for my bold attempts to head the EU?

Finally, after a long chat with myself, I realised that I am talking about the most powerful people in Europe. They are serious, intellectual people who most certainly got into politics in the first place for no personal gain other than the satisfaction of helping to vastly improve the lives of people in their home countries. They know it is serious business. They have no time for fun, laughter, banter and mickey-taking. Lives are at stake. I know that I am ready to run Europe – my goal is to make these people know it, too.

But why am I so supremely confident? (And know that I am.) Well, I am probably underrating myself a little here but I would say I am not quite in the elite category. But that is not a negative analysis. It is very much a positive and fantastic thing. While I possess the intellect and persuasive powers of the elite, the ability to lead and control the masses, I am also very much in touch with the common man, and that's what sets me apart from the hidden, well-protected, suit-wearing, drivel-ridden men of the EU.

There are many things I will do to serve the EU should my application be successful. As a brilliant example, I have huge plans surrounding one of the EU's biggest goals, which is to improve trade between member countries. As a fellow Brit, you will know that one of the most popular pastimes in this country is that of the noble car-boot sale. My contacts in Europe tell me that similar activities take place across the continent. What better way, then, than to bring nations together by holding international boot sales?

We all know that economies are struggling around the world, and European countries of all shapes and sizes are not spared. Even that weird wellie-shape of Italy and the Norwegian sperm. (Have you seen the Norwegian sperm? It really does look like one, sprawling right across the back of poor Sweden! I don't know *what* it's trying to do!)

My plan is to promote the idea of the European car-boot sale on a massive scale. I want travelling car-boot events where natives of each country tour around Europe as one mass convoy, virtually emptying their lands of people and vehicles, all the cars piled up with their own individual crap, setting up unbelievable numbers of square-miles of stalls and open boots and watch the locals of each country flock in their hundreds of thousands.

As we sit back and watch the huge success of these events, we can make a contest of it, *Bargain Hunt*-style, whereby the contestants (each EU nation) compete to make the most profit on any given event. The scores can be tallied up over the course of a car-boot season, like a league table, and the winning country gets the European Boot Award. The top individual performer within that country wins a seat in the EU.

This is just one of my many excellent and exciting ideas to boost an ailing European economy and to promote trade and entrepreneurialism among EU countries, among many other wonderful things. But I need you, Ms. Lambert, to get excited about Broadley versus Blair in a race for the Presidency. I ask you kindly to put my application forward to the decision-makers on the board of the EU. Please tell them I would be glad to meet any or all of the fellows and give a full three-hour presentation outlining my ideas fully. That shall be treated as my full interview before I am entered on to the ballot and elections begin.

Sarah, it is my time. It is Europe's time. 'EU' (pronounced 'you') won't regret it. In fact, upon meeting me, you may even exclaim:

"EU BEAUTY!!!" (And not just because of my looks.)

I look forward to hearing from you soon and leading Europe to some truly prosperous and glorious years ahead. All from the boot of my car.

Yours sincerely,

Your President-elect to-be, Sam Broadley

European Commission

5th November, 2009

Dear Mr. Broadley,

Thank you for your letter of 23rd October, to Sarah Lambert, who has asked me to reply on her behalf. The question of who will become President of the European Council will be resolved by a political decision taken at European Council level by the Member States of the European Union, and the Commission has no competence in this matter. I enclose herewith the extract from the Lisbon Treaty on the Election of the President of the European Council:

Article 15

5. The European Council shall elect its President, by a qualified majority, for a term of two and a half years, renewable once. In the event of an impediment or serious misconduct, the European Council can end the President's term of office in accordance with the same procedure.

We have, accordingly, forwarded your letter for the attention of the General-Secretariat of the Council of Ministers. The contact details, for future reference, are:

General-Secretariat of the Council

Yours sincerely,

Public Diplomacy

CONSILIUM

20th November, 2009

Dear Sir,

The office of the European Commission Representation in the United Kingdom passed your correspondence, received 4th November, on to the General-Secretariat of the Council of the European Union.

At their informal meeting in Brussels on 19th November, the Heads of State or Government reached a political agreement on the following appointments:

President of the European Council – Mr. Herman van Rompuy;

High Representative of the Union for Foreign Affairs and Security Policy – Ms. Catherine Ashton;

Secretary-General of the Council – Mr. Pierre de Boissieu.

The formal decisions on these appointments will be taken once the Treaty of Lisbon has entered force on 1st December 2009.

Yours faithfully,

The Public Information Service

Sam Broadley

Ipswich
Suffolk

2nd December, 2009

Dear Mr. Archie Norman,

I am writing to formally apply for the currently available position of **Chief Executive** of ITV.

Firstly, congratulations on your new role as Chairman. You were, in my opinion, absolutely the right man for the job as I did not apply. I decided not to approach ITV regarding the role due to other projects I have been working on. I have always known I was tailor-made for television (both sides of the camera), but I felt it was only fair to join a TV company once I could make a full commitment. And the good news for you is that time has come.

The good news for *me* is that ITV has struggled terribly to attract the best people for the position of CEO, and the search is still on. Your long-term remit is obvious: make better programmes, attract a bigger share of the audience, increase advertising revenue. But immediately, your job is to find the right man or woman (definitely a man: me) to front that role.

Let me quote you from a recent article I read during my research on you about your search for a CEO (in square brackets, you'll see my critique of the respective section).

"There have been a lot of public shenanigans over the last few months [correct]*, but I have a record of bringing in and developing*

top talent [true enough]. *I'm not going to be in a great hurry* [you should be]. "

Let me qualify my opinions. ITV has been a laughing stock. The BBC are the ones guffawing at the gaffes. Your extraordinary personal business achievements exude brilliance in spotting talent and nurturing flair into greatness. But, with respect, to say you will "take your time" is a miscalculation on your part, Mr. Norman. During what are tough times for this special broadcaster, you, in my humble yet great opinion, need to race along the roads and rails, across the seas and skies, to search for that perfect person to take the ITV family to where it should be: to the top of the televisual tree.

Fret not, though, Archie Norman, for this is where I, a marvellous media man, come in.

Hailing from a journalistic background (Home-learning Diploma, 2006), I am, just like you, an achiever. I achieve the things I set out to achieve, achieving things that can be classed among the greatest achievements among all the achievements of achievers everywhere. But I have yet, in my opinion, to achieve greatness. And that, Mr. Norman, is where we can help each other.

My experiences in television are probably greater than yours. I am media-savvy, having appeared on television many times, both locally here in East Anglia and nationally (UK). If you talk about pressure, try going on a live television game show. I did. 'Twas in the spring of '04. *The 24-Hour Quiz*, its name. ITV, in fact. I was answering trivia questions under brutal conditions in front of millions of viewers. Many would've crumbled early on. Not me. I fell apart much closer to the winning-post.

But I don't simply want to perform. I would be wasted by only transforming people's viewing experiences for the good. I also have outstanding business acumen. The two, most would say, cannot go together. Well, excuse me, but I beg to differ and so do. I am the exception to the saying, 'Jack of all trades, master of none'. I am known to those close as 'Sam of two trades, *ring*master of *both.*'

If chosen, I am going to transform ITV into the number-one force, not in five years', two years' or even 12 months' time. I'm talking within four weeks from the beginning of my project as CEO. How? Simple. I am going to quite literally run the show.

The first three weeks from my appointment will be completely dedicated to learning everything inside-out about each and every current ITV1 show. I will delve into every nook and cranny of every programme from sunrise to sunset and beyond, getting to know each and every member of each and every team on the most intimate of levels. Why?

Because I am going to present every single ITV1 programme.

When you have picked your jaw up from the floor, please read on, for this is quite a serious project and one I have thought long and hard about. It is not fanciful or whimsical, it is feasible and well worth doing. I am capable. I have the knowledge, the respect, the draw, the stature, the confidence, the charisma, the presence, the poise and the looks to present any one given show. Team that up with my youth, energy, drive, fitness, power, strength, stamina, endurance and looks, then why *couldn't* I present every show going?

My day will start by opening *GMTV* at 6am, present it right through to *Lorraine Kelly* (which will be me), then *The Jeremy Kyle Show (The Sam Broadley Show)*, after which it's off to *This Morning*, then a swift jog across to the *Loose Women* studio, before nipping over to broadcast the all-important lunchtime news bulletin to the nation, followed by *Dickinson's Real Deal (Broadley's Real Deal)* and subsequently *The Alan Titchmarsh Show (The Sam Broadley Show)*. Then I get a good break while we play a *Midsomer Murders* re-run (which I'll probably watch), before it's back on for *Goldenballs*. Then it's an hour for both the local and national news (I'll probably have to present these from the same studio with different backdrops), before appearances in both *Emmerdale* and *Coronation Street* (as different characters). I must be ready to present the next action, which on Wednesday nights is European football and could be anywhere on the continent. Luckily, the soaps are pre-recorded, which gives me time to hop on a plane and get there. Then it's back for more news (I might have to do this from Europe), before finally gracing *Benidorm*.

A hectic schedule, I'm sure you'll agree, but the rewards are genuinely endless. We will hold an international press conference to announce my inauguration where we will tell everyone listening of the new CEO's hands-on approach to running the ITV company. They will be surprised at the commitments I am promising to make, but I will explain to them what I will explain to you: this is all for the future of ITV.

If I take on this daunting task of presenting all programming whilst simultaneously running the business, this will not only save a great deal of money by sacking all of the current presenters while retaining me on a single going-rate salary, the talk of the world will be so great that I guarantee the viewing figures will increase by thousands of percent!

Archie, come and speak to me. We'll have a serious chat about this seemingly farcical idea. You'll see what I'm like in the flesh, smile at my bouncy demeanour and think to yourself, *You know what? This might just work...*

You'll watch me turn around ITV and churn up the BBC.

I look forward to hearing from you and subsequently presenting my ideas to you and my programmes to the world.

Yours sincerely,

Sam Broadley

4th January, 2010

Dear Sam,

Thank you for your letter applying for the position of Chief Executive at ITV.

I was interested to read your 'Day One' plans, but at this time, I regret we will be unable to take the matter further.

Thank you again for taking the time to write to me.

Archie Norman

Chairman

Prof. Sam Broadley

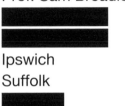

Ipswich
Suffolk

6th January, 2010

Dear Professor Edward Acton,

I am writing to formally apply for the currently available position of **Head Climate Scientist** of the University of East Anglia.

My letter is targeted at you, Professor, as the Vice Chancellor of the UEA, because I know you wish to resolve the debacle of your climate team and those pesky leaked emails at your earliest opportunity. I'm writing to appease the situation and, quite literally, save the day.

My biggest passion in life is weather. I bloody love the weather. I love the sun. I love the rain. I love the hail. I love the snow. I love the lightning and subsequent thunder. I'm also a fan of the wind. Ultimately, as a scientist, I love learning about the ways in which weather patterns, both on a day-to-day basis and over the ages, affect the existence of life – particularly mine and those of some of my fellow humans, most animals and a few plants.

Like yourselves at UEA, my main concern is climate change. Despite the cynics and conspiracy theorists of this our battered world, I am convinced (thanks to my extensive findings) that the climate is changing dramatically as a direct result of the destructive actions of Man (and Woman – she is not exempt from my criticism). The people of the world need to understand this, and the great work the gang at UEA has done and continues to do is vital in proving we are right and getting that message across.

Sadly, the actions of the previous Head Climate Scientist, Professor Phil Jones, in doubting his own work and allowing those scandalous emails to be leaked was, putting it lightly, a disgrace. The team at UEA is the most highly-respected in the world (which is quite impressive for a bunch who dwell in Norwich). Their work should never be doubted. If they are doubting themselves, the world will continue to doubt and lose faith in the intelligent people of this world, the likes of you and I.

You've had some seriously bad press of late. The world is turning against you and people of your ilk. You'll continue to watch the people batter you like a gale against a washing line if you don't salvage your tattered reputation. You know yourself it's time to bring in a man (or woman, but definitely a man) to blow in some fresh air to calm the storm. You're after a man (a man) to save the world from utter disaster resulting in the complete extinction of life.

This is where I, a scientific saviour of souls, come in.

My latest research shows that it is snowing heavily, as I type. In fact, heavier than at any time since (my) records began. These unprecedented levels of snowfall will have the critics guffawing, shouting with glee: "Global Warming?? Bah! I told you those daft scientists were wrong! I told you it was scaremongering!" This idiocy of the masses is clearly further adding to the pressures on us as scientists. If only these simpletons realised what the extra-cold weather *actually* means: Mother Nature is playing with our emotions.

Mother Nature has fallen out of love with Mankind. She's had enough of the way in which we have developed over the millennia.

And who can blame Her? Generation after generation of savages. Wars, terror, invasions, greed, wreaking poverty on one another. All this in Her own garden. She's fed up with us all and decided it's time to start afresh without us. She has begun to change weather patterns on the quiet with a view to wiping us out.

She underrated our intelligence, though, as a species, for She has witnessed Mankind work out what's happening, then watched us react with panic about rising temperatures and sea levels. She's not taking anything for granted, not going to sit back and watch us discover a way of conquering the elements. This snow malarkey is a *decoy*. It's to get us thinking, "Actually, this place ain't warming up after all – let's build a snowman!"

Then, when we're all off making snow-angels for the next couple of years, BANG! Out goes the Ozone, in come the sunrays, thump goes the San Andreas Fault and all its cousins around the world, up goes Yellowstone, and finally, oops – there's goes Life.

Drastic? Of course. An apocalypse is no summer picnic. And it's vital we don't turn our backs on it.

The statements I make may appear extraordinary, such as personifying Mother Nature, portraying Her as a some kind of vengeful god. I accept that. But I am a maverick scientist. I do things differently from the other professors. Rest assured, though, my methods are the soundest around, hence my findings as per above. There is not another scientist on our green Earth who could have realised we are in a direct battle of wits with Mother Nature Herself. This is a conscious war, make no mistake.

What I want from you... let me rephrase that: what the *world needs* from you is to meet me and let me spend two-hours-and-forty-two minutes presenting my methods of practice and my subsequent conclusions. You will want me on your team. I will rally your troops, reinstate their passion, vigour and determination to prove to our people that this war is real and that we've got to take it to Her.

I also have a Plan B. In case we are unsuccessful in proving to people that we are in a fight to the death, my team have been working on something in the event of potentially catastrophic sea levels. Here in the secret fields of Suffolk, we are, under my authority, in the process of building a gargantuan machine, measuring 560x780x6m in mass, designed to drain colossal amounts of seawater from... well, the sea.

Using a specially-designed *transporter*, this beast is taken to an agreed location just off Felixstowe beach where we will store huge capsules into which the seawater will be poured through a big funnel. Attached to the underside of each of these heat-proof capsules are eight jet engines powerful enough to send them all the way to the Sun. And that's exactly where they're going: the Sun. By doing this, we will not only decrease sea-levels but cleverly use that seawater to actually *put out* just a little bit of the Sun's red-hot fire, thus inevitably lowering temperatures slightly, icecaps not melting but reforming and sea-levels dipping even further. With time, as we get closer and closer to our ideal temperature, there will be less and less requirement for the use of my innovative invention, which, by the way, is called:

'SAM'S SENDER OF SEA TO THE SUN'.

I suggest with all my might that you allow me to breeze in and raise the temperature of this debate. Like a light at night, I promise you I will create a hell of a storm among the scientific world. You will stand aghast, quaking as you watch me, a seasoned campaigner, erupt with gusto and display a whirlwind of ideas. You will hail me as a hero, and that snow joke. Like a jet-stream and with fire in my belly, I will rain on any doubter's parade. I will come at the world like a tidal-wave, avalanching anyone who dares to question our deep philosophy:

Life
Is
For
Ever.

Get me in. Survival of the human race depends on me – 'weather' you like it or not.

I look forward to meeting with you and thrashing out my plans to bash Mother Nature before She bashes us.

Yours sincerely,

Professor Sam D. Broadley

University of East Anglia

2nd February, 2010

Dear Professor Broadley,

The Vice Chancellor has asked me to acknowledge your letter of 6th January (received 1st February) and to thank you for your comments, which have been noted.

As you will be aware, the matters you raise are the subject of a police enquiry and the Independent Review being led by Sir Muir Russell and I have no doubt that they will be thoroughly investigated. The University is committed to making the recommendations from the Review public and will take any action that is appropriate as a result of the Review's findings.

Yours sincerely,

Senior Assistant Registrar

Sam Broadley

██████████
██████████

Ipswich
Suffolk

██████████

14th September, 2010

Dear Mr. Jeremy Clarkson,

I am writing to formally apply for the surprisingly available position of **The Stig** on your hit BBC television series *Top Gear*.

I say surprisingly because it was a shock to me that a man such as Ben Collins, as he is now well and truly globally known, decided all of a sudden that he wanted the world to know who he was. My feeling is that he enjoyed the ongoing speculation and mutterings among the press and his many fans as to who he really was until the point where his head got far too big for his helmet and so it had to come off for all to see. He wanted to bask in the glory of being Britain's best-loved driver of a mechanically-propelled vehicle. Even though, ironically, he wouldn't be any more.

Of course, naturally, there is money involved. It isn't just a case of Ben satisfying his ego; there's also the small matter of a book deal and a spin-off television series. Well, who can blame him? I can, for one.

What gets me, Jeremy, what really grinds against my skull like a grinder on a head of bone, is that the man was worshipped much like a god by myself and millions of others. Comparing him to a divine being may seem a little dramatic, but I'm right.

You think of the billions of God-worshippers around the world. What do you think would happen if He threatened to reveal Himself, face-to-many-faces, as the creator of Earth and Man?

Well, obviously, people wouldn't really want it. They might say they do now but I know they wouldn't if they actually got the option, and the reason they wouldn't is because they wouldn't know how to deal with it. What would they do? What would they say? How would they account for all their sins? A measly confession session and a vicar saying, "Ah, never mind, learn for next time," wouldn't suffice now, for The Man is there in front of their eyes.

Being The Stig, in many respects, is no different. Millions of us have debated endlessly about who the man behind the visor is, the yearning to know the identity of our idol, the man who we most want to *be* in the world. Our desperation to delve into the threads of our god lead to The Stig declaring his wish, his insistence, his ultimate will to reveal himself to his people.

That was the moment I did not want to know. Fear gripped me like a vice around my ball-twins. "Please stay as The Stig!" I prayed. It didn't work. The BBC failed in their attempt to thwart his efforts, the courtroom judge granting the man's wish to rid himself of his godly whites and declare himself as… as a two-bit amateur racing driver. Good one, Ben. Way to impress upon your people.

You may be wondering, Jeremy, why I have, in fact, spent so much of my letter of application talking of the previous Stig and my newly-found scorn for him. It's quite simple: the job is one that any man given the ultimate honour of being blessed with should be in love with for life and beyond. There is simply something mentally wrong with a man who would even consider giving up such prestige for a little bit of short-term fame, which is all it'll be. Ben Collins is mentally wrong. I'm not a doctor and never likely to be, but I know this to be a medical fact.

Now this literal idiot has moved on, it's time for you, Jeremy, to find yourself a Stig you believe in, the world believes in and, most importantly, a Stig who knows he is the most important man on the planet AS THE STIG ONLY.

This is where I, a divinely driven supernatural spectacle, come in.

Every man of sane mind wants to be The Stig. Most men would kill another man to become The Stig. That seems a bit far, although maybe I'd assassinate a few properly evil people if it meant getting the role. That'd be like a double success. Or maybe I could run them over when I start the job!

Passion alone is not enough to get this gig, of course. The New Stig needs much more than that. So what have I got? Two things for you to consider for starters…

First off, I am an outstanding driver of any conveyance. Aged 29, I passed my driving test in March previous. That's ever so late in life, isn't it?! Whilst at first glance this makes me inexperienced, a closer look will of course tell you that it gives me that inevitable boy-racer confidence but also the maturity my advanced years (in test-passing terms) naturally brings. Now *that's* an asset.

Second off, I am a showman. If you are a man who happens to naturally doubt things in life, doubt this not. I am nothing without a crowd. If I'm short of a fan club, I am no man. Currently, I am no man. But being The Stig will change that. I've never lied in a job application and I'm not going to start now: my newly-developed status as a god to millions is likely to go to my head. However, my knowledge of the importance of the role as guidance for my people will keep my feet firmly on the pedals.

As a precaution, though, I have decided to take no chances. When you employ me and I inevitably go on to become the most profound and publicly sought-after Stig ever, I will deal with the fame by releasing a single whilst continuing to safeguard my identity. I've not gone into any detail in my mind at this stage with regards to the song choice, sleeve design or marketing (it probably won't need any marketing, in actual fact; it'll be snapped up by just about every person almost immediately through word of mouth), but an early consideration is *Baby, You Can't Drive My Car* (I'm very protective of my vehicles). As I say, it's an early idea but, although it might be a slightly muffled version what with having my helmet on and all, it's a cracking choice of cover, I think you'll agree.

As I have touched on several times, I am aware of the responsibility the position of The Stig holds. The millions that rely on him for direction can be extremely daunting for many a man to say the very least. Not for me, however. I understand the power I will have and I will use it to positive effect only and most certainly will not let it consume me, and nor will I allow, other than entering the music industry, such power to affect my humble nature.

I will be, though, be building Stig Churches across the length and breadth of the country for My followers to worship Me in. People everywhere will have access to a House of Stig near to their homes where they can go and pray or give thanks for their blessings that The Stig has given them. It is likely that, as The New Stig (as He is likely to be dubbed) evolves and becomes a probable omnipresent, Stig Churches will start popping up across Europe and other parts of the world.

I understand the importance of giving My people the stability in their lives of knowing there is a figurehead for them and that I am He. I am aware, through no fault of My own, that I will become perhaps the most important religious leader on Earth, not because I'll be the lead representative of a god – I will be *The* God.

Jeremy, you know yourself that *Top Gear* is some of the finest television programming of all time. It would be a true shame for it to go under because of the selfish moves of one man. The (at the time) most important man. Make The Stig loved again. Give Me the job of my dreams to be The Stig of My people's dreams. Watch the show grow and your audience rocket. I can even guarantee that with you as My number-one disciple, your own personal fan base will double. Minimum.

I challenge you to select Me and then let's **GO, GO, GO!!!**

I very much look forward to your reply and driving together to take *Top Gear* into a new gear and transforming the religious face of this our great world.

Yours sincerely,

Sam Broadley

PS: I don't currently own a crash helmet, but to show you an example of me looking anonymous, I've included a photo for your enjoyment. Enjoy!

Sam Broadley

Ipswich
Suffolk

14th September, 2010

Dear Mr. Simon Cowell,

I am writing to formally apply for the position of *X Factor* **Judge**.

It has been well documented across the media (and you will have heard) that our Cheryl Cole (Tweedy?) has been suffering from malaria and has taken a break from work. And so she should. It's serious. But it has of course left you with a headache of your own, not helped by the further departure of Dannii Minogue after landing herself with a pregnancy.

My understanding is that Cheryl is well on the mend, which makes me very pleased. I am in love with the girl (please don't tell her because that would be embarrassing for us both!), despite her violent past, and I am happy she is getting better. But she is not yet ready for work. You need an interim judge.

It has recently been brought to my attention that you are also at an advanced stage of planning to bring in a fifth judge, whether that be this series or next. So two judges down and you want to *increase* the bench! Wow, you really are in a pickle!

Names of the potential forthcoming fifth judge are already subject to much speculation among the press and public. Huge music stars, such as Geri Halliwell and Robbie Williams, to name but two, are being bandied about. I must admit that I, as a huge fan of the show, have been very excited by the prospect of such heroes joining an already excellent line-up. This would definitely take the programme to a new level, making it hugely more successful than ever before.

Well, that was my view until recently. I care about the show as if it were my own, and as a result, I have thought long and hard about who should be the next judge to grace the great judges' bench. Having calmed down from the initial wild excitement of potentially recruiting a huge musical legend (which took several days), a more logical thought process has taken place. My personal view (and my opinions are usually the right ones) is now that your plan is going down completely the wrong route, Simon. Your job as a customer-facing man is to connect with your public, to have something that you can relate to them with. You will fail to achieve this with yet another massive personality on board.

What you desperately, *desperately* need is a total unknown. A complete nobody. Someone with absolutely no respect in the world from anyone anywhere.

This is where I, a man unrespected everywhere, come in.

Please know, though, that this is not to put myself down. Yes, no-one holds me in any kind of regard, and yes, no-one has shown the slightest interest in any of my opinions on any conceivable subject, but this is to our huge, huge advantage for *X Factor*. No-one knows me and so no-one has any pre-informed opinions me. That means I'm coming on to the show with a blank slate, as a non-establishment music-lover. That's all. I am *one of them.*

You see, as an average man, all average men, women and children across the country will relate to me, thus trust me and believe in me. And there are a hell of a lot of average people out there.

In this age of financial disparity, bankers, politicians, businessmen and even celebrities of all types are looked upon with scorn. Despite recent successes, Mr. Cowell, you would be foolish to think you are exempt from public criticism and are not subject to mistrust from the masses. You need to reconnect with your public – and you need me to do the connecting.

But why me? As suggested, there are loads of irrelevant people in this country. What makes me so averagely special? Several factors, really.

At 29, I am neither young nor old. I'm at a stage in life where I am in touch with modern music and all the latest crazes, yet I have a deep appreciation for times gone by and the revolutionary periods, for stars such as The Beatles, The Bee Gees, Boy George and Beethoven.

I also have a link with *X Factor* itself. As a singing contestant, I am a twice-failure. Two attempts to make it to the big time have been thwarted during the preliminary round, much to my utter disgust. I am too good a singer for that to have happened. My plan was, actually, to become a thrice-loser by challenging again in May of this year. However, I have decided against it, preferring instead to apply for the job of Judge, which is where my number-one talent sits, as you will see post-contestants' performances once you take me on.

On the subject of my judging talents, I am excellent. This is proven, not only in my musical tastes but in several walks of life. A good example is through my friendship with an ugly man close to me. Due to his awful looks, he has little confidence with the women. And rightly so. I don't wish to name him, but, between you and I only, he resembles the offspring of Pinocchio and Quasimodo chewing on a maggot-infested lemon after an allergic reaction to a bee sting. (I am fully aware of the inconsistency of my analogy, for not only are Pinocchio and Quasimodo both male, the former is a wooden puppet, therefore any plans to make a baby between them are likely to prove fruitless.)

But people like him should never lose faith in their pulling power. And, to his credit, he didn't. But he did call upon my judging talents. We spent an evening together in several pubs and a nightclub in the town of Ipswich, purely in pursuit of suitable women for my butt-ugly friend. He quite literally had no idea whom he should be targeting. My job was to, as an expert, select the very, very few numbers of females that may be willing to talk to him with a view to successfully forming a long-term relationship with one of them.

Despite it being a humungous long shot, I systematically judged and discounted several thousand unsuspecting contestants until I'd whittled it down to just twelve remaining girls who, in my opinion, were suitable to be approached. Armed with just a single question as his opener provided by myself (which was "Would you prefer to fornicate with a delicious-looking evil murderer or an ugly but lovely man?"), he bravely walked up to each. I am very proud to say that not once did he get laughed at, abused, ridiculed or slapped. Even though none ended in mutual love, it can be classed as a magnificent success. Results speak for themselves, Simon. That is excellent judging.

What I ask of you, Sir Simon, is to meet me face-to-face so you can do what you do best – judge. Judge me, and whilst judging me, I shall judge you to perfection, which will have the desired knock-on effect of you judging me as an excellent judge of people, at which point you will judge me to be an outstanding judge for the judging panel on *X Factor's* judging bench.

I have some outstanding ideas for the up-and-coming fifth category for the show, including over-85s and four-legged animals. In such untapped and underrated markets, there really is some unbelievable quality, some truly terrific talent.

Once I have taken over from Cheryl pending her recovery, there's no way you'll want to get rid of me. This extra position you are creating is magnificent timing, for you will slot me right in as a permanent fixture. I can even see you, in time, demoting yourself as the main judge and allowing me to step up!

I have already thought ahead to the round before the live shows where you take contestants to your beautiful place in Los Angeles, Louis flies his gang to his mansion in Ireland, while Dannii and Cheryl jet-set their groups to their equally stunning dwellings of Europe. I have also thought about the co-judges you all have alongside you at this stage, the likes of Dannii having her sister, you entwined with Sunita and Louis cosying up with Ronan. Well, my lot will have to make do with my end-terrace two-bed in Ipswich. It's a new-build with a garden so it'll do the job. As for my co-judge, that'll be my younger brother, Luke. He's not famous but he will be once I've aired him on X Factor, which is the aim (I promised him fame one day).

Mr. Cowell, I very much look forward to receiving written correspondence from you regarding my application with a view to meeting you over the coming days. I know auditions are well underway now as the pre-recorded shows are currently airing so sooner rather than later please so you can get me in and announce my arrival to our public in time for the latter stages.

Si, get me in and watch the ratings rise higher than your waistband (which is significantly high). I can't wait to work alongside you and discover the next fine talent Britain has to offer, whether it be an 18-year-old hot lad, a 20-year-old sizzling chick, a 92-year-old vocal vixen or a beautifully melodic sheep.

Yours sincerely,

Sam Broadley

PS: You're probably intrigued as to my looks and how suitable my appearance is for television. I have, therefore, included a little photograph of myself in an appropriate guise to give you an idea. I look wonderfully judgemental, I'm sure you'll agree.

Sam Broadley

███████████

███████████

Ipswich

Suffolk

███████████

7th February, 2011

Dear Prime Minister David Cameron,

I am writing to formally apply for the currently available position of **Downing Street Director of Communications**.

Before I get on to writing about myself, as is necessary when trying to earn a place in Government by way of letter, I'd like to express a few words of opinion on my predecessor (to be) (hopefully).

Andrew (informally Andy) Coulson was an outstanding servant to you and your party. His resignation did shake you, although it was not entirely unsurprising to you nor I given his unfortunate downfall at the *News of the World* over the phone-tapping scandal. When you came out and gave a statement of regret and disappointment at his decision to resign, I saw nothing but regret and disappointment in your eyes. I can read a man. I read you, Mr. Cameron, like an easy-to-read pamphlet. I enjoyed the informative pamphlet.

Sadly, Coulson's past came back to haunt him, as I knew it would. I am a man of experience, and experience has told me that bums get bitten by old, hungry gremlins who you think you've shaken off but inevitably haven't. If anything, Coulson should have foreseen this and used his supposed communication skills to manipulate public opinion in his favour. I won't suggest how I would have done that – I'm not daft enough to put it on to paper and wait for my letter to be intercepted by some oik at Royal Mail and then suddenly my name's across the press. No way. I will tell you in person at the interview (once I've carried out a check for bugs; I'm not an idiot).

Whilst you yourself have publicly expressed your thanks for the fantastic job Coulson did for you, you may secretly regret the decision to hire him based on the controversy it brought and his inevitable premature end. I wouldn't expect you to admit that and I wouldn't even ask you to. It's a respect thing.

I think you now know, though, what with the less-than-popular Coalition Government and all the things bolted to it, your next publicist needs to be free of the associated hullabaloo.

This is where I, a publicity, PR and press person with panache, come in.

That's right: panache. It's a good word (pronounced *pan-ash*). I only recently learnt it, but it was made for me, such is my flamboyance among people.

I have great experience among the press and all forms of media, Prime Minister. I have been interviewed on television and radio for charity events I have organised and taken part in, for instance. Of course, I've been delighted to have raised vital funds for very important causes, but it's really all about raising my own profile, which I have successfully achieved in some very localised parts of the country. (Please don't tell the charities about my real motives – they get a bit funny about it. Selfish of them, really, considering all I've done for them.) I have written journalistic articles, designed posters for events and also entered countless competitions with well-known national magazines, such as *Take a Break*.

Some of these may seem small-fry to the likes of a Government minister (the Prime one in particular), but please understand why I network with the small media: it's because by playing with the small fish, I get to sneak up on the big fish and tickle their fancies to put smiles on their faces, get them excited about me and win their hearts. We're all in the same pond, Mr. Cameron. You just have to know which way the current's flowing and swim that way. (I am aware, thank you, that ponds don't often have currents.) I am a strong swimmer (not literally; I'm actually rubbish, but you get my drift (excuse the pun)).

Upon success in my pursuit of the job of my dreams, I will be implementing a number of my pre-planned plans. You see, I don't just consider my role to be simply using my contacts in the press. I envisage playing a major role in revamping your public image. You have begun an immensely tough tenure as the boss of Britain, and whilst your actions are necessary, they are making you unpopular.

With that in mind, I have a plan to overhaul two key areas of your appearance/persona: I will make you physically strong and I will make you cool.

I have already consulted a top Ipswich-based personal trainer and together we have analysed your frame and shape. We are both agreed that you appear reasonably fit for a man of your middle-range years, yet your build is too slight. Thanks to a high-intensity weights training programme designed specifically for you, we will having you looking like an outside toilet building within 12 weeks. A physically strong man makes for a mentally strong leader. Plus you'll look sexy.

It's vital I make you cool. You are not naturally, with all due respect, a cool man. Your posh background automatically put paid to that. I think it's fair to say you won the election race by default in that you are slightly cooler than Nick Clegg and way cooler than Gordon Brown (no effort necessary for the latter). But that's something to work on. We need to get you down with the kids; hip, phat, diggin', dabomb. Cool gets you respect, and respect gets you votes. After all these cuts, you ain't gonna get the votes without the coolness and the respect.

In order to achieve the status of cool, I will be exploiting my media contacts to embark on a PR campaign to show our public the *real* you (or what *will* be the real you once I've taught you cool ways in which to conduct yourself – I'm thinking things like adding a bit of Cockney rhyming slang to your speech, maybe adding some braids to your hair and also learning to do a little bit of ad-lib rapping to throw at Ed Miliband during Prime Minister's Questions… He might ask, "Prime Minister, do you not think these cuts are just too brutal?" to which you may reply, "The name's Dave C, Westminster's MC, I gotta cut the deficit cos y'all caused us some sh**, yo, respec').

I'm going to see to it that your campaign covers all target markets out there. You'll appear in magazines such as *Hello!, Nuts, National Geographic, Horse & Hound* and *The Beano*. The idea is to show the nation that you can communicate with people from all walks of life on their level. I will see to it that you appear on some of TV's most popular shows. You will guest-present *Never Mind the Buzzcocks*, become a comedy panellist on *Mock the Week*, head *Blue Peter* and you'll appear in *Coronation Street* as yourself. I also have a plan to make you the next Stig on *Top Gear* – you will be the best one ever and your identity will only be released during the run-up to the next election, at which point your popularity will be through the roof! You will be the coolest Prime Minister ever! Cooler even than John Major ever was.

Prime Minister, I love everything to do with the Conservative Party.

Everything. I have a conservative mindset (though maverick also), I love conservatories (my mum and dad have just had one built on to the back of their house, actually; it looks very nice) and I really enjoy conversations (which makes me the ideal publicist, surely).

When you invite me for interview, Boss Man, you will see for yourself that I have a natural gift when it comes to turning people into what they want to be and what they need to be. You can't help where you've come from but you can help where you go. *I* can help you on your journey to rule Great Britain long-term and, later, the world.

You've heard of Optimum Prime, the greatest and most powerful of all the Transformers. Well I will transform you so you will be known simply as:

OPTIMUM PRIME MINISTER – the coolest and most powerful being on Earth.

I look forward very much to meeting you and working with you to make this world your own.

Yours sincerely,

Sam Broadley

Sam Broadley

██████████████

██████████████

Ipswich

Suffolk

██████████

21st February, 2011

Dear Sirs,

I am writing to formally apply for the available position of **Presenter of Football Programming** at Sky Sports.

I am writing to formally apply for the available position of **Football Commentator** at Sky Sports.

That's right: one letter, both roles. As a member of the male gender (don't be fooled by my unisexual first name), I am blessed with common sense, and common sense tells me to combine two applications for two currently-available roles within just the one letter. Common sense. To make it perfectly clear, I am applying for both jobs because I *want both* jobs. Not one or the other. Both. Although if you were to offer one or the other, I'd take it without argument.

These jobs, you'll remember, became available after a huge scandal of sexism within the workplace involving Richard Keys and Andy Gray (as the perpetrators, not the victims). As the main men of Sky Sports for 20 years and with records as clean as a freshly-wiped worktop by the soft hand of a loving wife, it came as a huge shock to me to hear of their engagement in sexist conversation, banter and bullying. But why? (Why did they do it, not why was is it a shock to me – that's obvious: because it's bad.)

One can only presume two things. First, they're utterly consumed within the football world, the working man's game where men worship the sport invented by the English for the world. They cheer, they chant, they jeer, they jaunt, they drink, they shout, they eat pies, they tell their missus to "shut it" cos the footy's on. Second, they have money and power and see women as sex objects.

Now, of course women are sex objects. Of *course* they are. They bloody well are. Look at 'em. Gorgeous, some of 'em. What man of a heterosexual inclination wouldn't say, "Cor, yeah, she's a physically attractive adult female I would like to get to know better with a view to enjoying a physical relationship within, possibly more..."?

But women are so much more than that these days. They have *brains*! It's true, they do. Once, our cavemen predecessors would display their dominance by dragging their women round by the hair. But the women evolved to *learn* that if they didn't like being pulled around as such, they could have *haircuts*.

Later on in the evolutionary process, up to the times of the 1960s, a woman's role was very much within the home, first as a wife involving cooking, cleaning, washing, ironing, hoovering, bed-making, gardening, chimney-sweeping, bathing the dog, looking pretty ready for when the man got home from work. Added to that later, baby-maker and subsequent baby-looker-afterer. *Added*. Not *in place of*. *Added*. This is where the term 'multi-tasking' came from. So over many thousands of years, their brains had got *bigger*.

Now we find in modern-day times that women have chosen to go to *work*! Build *careers*! I am a younger man of 30 yet that even seems strange to me. We have enough men in our world to cover all the jobs out there so why do we need women other than for the list provided within the 1960s paragraph? But I understand that as women's intelligence has improved and continues to get closer to men's, so has their right to think, work, vote and have opinions on a variety of subjects, political and otherwise. Football seems a bit far, but it's a new world and I for one embrace it and welcome females of all ages and varieties to join in with what is the greatest game on Earth.

You'll have noticed that up until now, I have spoken not of myself but only of the role of the female in modern society compared to the olden days. Well actually, I *am* speaking of myself. Not because I'm a female. I'm a male through and through, as stated at the top of this letter. Nothing feminine about me at all (apart from when I played the role of Dame Sparkles in a pantomime at Christmas time last gone when I was ever so camp!). I'm speaking of myself in that I'm proving to you that I believe in a modern world where we all mingle joyously, regardless of sex, race, age, religious beliefs, socio-economic standing and, yes, even intelligence. Thick people are people too.

As for my skills for the two jobs I am applying for, I strongly believe I am the man you are looking for. My knowledge of football is second to none. As an Ipswich Town supporter, I have experienced both the high-flying times of the Premiership and also the lower-flying times of the second tier (but no lower than that so please do not ask me to present or commentate on football matches unworthy of my pedigree).

My presenting skills are, I'm told, nothing short of top-class. This was an opinion offered to me by a schoolteacher once after a presentation and was duly award a grade B. In addition to that experience, I have had a number of public-facing roles, including retail, call-centres (not strictly facing, but you get what I mean) and also stage work (voluntary).

146

I mentioned earlier about playing the role of Dame in panto. I'd like to clarify that although I enjoyed the part very much, my first choice of attire on my debut Sky Sports appearance would probably not involve a massive dress, size 11 heels, a wig and a faceful of make-up. Having said that, it would in some way be embracing the idea that women should be more involved in heading sports-related programmes. I'd probably be prettier than Gabby Logan. I'd definitely be prettier than Claire Balding. I already am. I would be willing to wear the aforementioned.

As for my commentary skills, well, it's what I'm probably best at, alongside presenting. My dad loves watching football and he also loves listening to my commentary. Usually, when we're watching the footy together, he'll turn the sound off, put on a pre-recorded track of a stadium full of people cheering and ask me to commentate, which I duly do. I enjoy it and so does my dad.

It is important for me to clarify that I want both jobs. I want to be Presenter *and* Commentator. I can perform both roles. Apart from me being naturally gifted for both presenting and commentating, I want to prove to all women out there that men, too, are evolving. We, too, can multi-task. Despite what they may think, they've actually got some catching-up to do before they reach our levels of brainpower. But I genuinely want them to enjoy trying. They should never stop believing and I will support them always with pats on the head as they continue to walk through glue and treacle to make their way in what was once dubbed by well-known soul singer James Brown and, later, Mary Byrne on *X Factor* as "A Man's World".

Good luck to them all, I say. No matter what those dinosaurs Keys and Gray think.

I look forward to receiving a reply from you in due course with a view to taking over the reins at Sky Sports and moving us into a new multi-gender (or at least double-gender) era in football.

LET'S SAY **NO** TO SEXISM!!!!!

Yours faithfully,

Sam Broadley

Sam Broadley

████████████

████████████

Ipswich

Suffolk

████████

6th June, 2011

Dear Mr. John Lipsky,

I am writing to formally apply for the currently available position of **Managing Director** of the International Monetary Fund.

I've wanted this job for bloody ages. Finally I get the chance to apply (and I'm taking that chance), but it's a shame I'm having to do it under these circumstances. I refuse to go into detail of how this role has become available (you're already aware). I just want you to know that I planned on making a move really soon anyway, regardless of it being vacant or not.

You see, I am the best man for this job, better even than Dominique Strauss-Kahn was when he was there. My aim in this letter is to prove that if you had have heard of me two months ago, you'd have sacked Strauss-Kahn in any case.

Currently, you're Acting Managing Director. It's a worthy role and I want to offer my deep thanks to you right now as I type for the great work you are undoubtedly doing in stabilising what has been a rocky organisation of late. Your efforts are truly appreciated by me and many other esteemed scholars around the world. I do hope you're not getting too comfy in the big chair, though, Mr. Lipsky, because don't forget I'm looking to park my clever bottom there very soon! I speak in jest, of course, but I do mean it.

The IMF is at the forefront of everything financial in the world. It's the fulcrum from which 187 nations play their international financial games with one another. Essentially, we're all paying into a pot and when we need a loan, we borrow from it. It's a lovely system in which everyone benefits. Of course, some countries take the French kiss (to put it politely), but you expect some of that and so you make sure they suffer. In a nice way.

187. Sounds a lot, doesn't it? And it is. But it's not enough. This community of countries is such a wonderful organism that the whole world should be involved. But the whole is not. There are some who are too stubborn to enter into such a family, including Monaco, Andorra and Liechtenstein. Whilst they aren't what you'd call powerhouses on the world stage, they are vital to keep the funds topped up.

North Korea is another, but you wouldn't expect such an arrogant and deluded country to get involved in friendly fiscal frolics with us boys. They have delusions of grandeur. I see them as a bit like Oriental Amish: inter-reliant and all do the same things.

Then we have Vatican City. Built for and run by the Catholics. They felt it necessary, such is their religious dominance throughout the world, to be declared their own independent country by nicking a bit of Italy. A bit arrogant, but they achieved it so who am I to argue. I would have appreciated it, though, if they could have at least joined the IMF to show they are actually interested in talking to the rest of the world. Plus they've got an ungodly amount of cash we do with.

If I am successful, Mr. Lipsky, in my bid to be voted in as Managing Director of the IMF, my first target (of many, let me tell you) will be to get every country to sign up so we can share the cash around.

The titchy countries like cute little Andorra and sweet baby Lichtenstein won't take much persuading. The way I will approach this is to send in ground troops (from the IMF Army that I will be creating, consisting of the adult offspring of each member-country's representatives – if their offspring are still children, the reps will have to go themselves and take their wives) and take two or possibly three of their most stunning mountains as hostages. They will wrap them up in explosives, phone the countries' respective leaders and say that they will only release the mountains from capture if they sign up to the IMF. They will definitely do it because the mountains are pretty much all they've got to attract anyone there.

As for Monaco, well, they haven't got any mountains, but it's alright because I'm what's known among high-rollers as a super-gambler. My plan is to enter each casino and, one by one, wipe the floor with them using my incredible skills on the poker table and slot machines. When they are close to bankruptcy, I will offer all the money back, minus my travelling expenses, if they sign up to the IMF. They're bound to agree, such is the country's reliance upon the godly sin of gambling. (By the way, I know I could make a personal fortune by being a super-gambler, but my quest in life is not one of self-interest – I want to better the world and *all* its people.)

North Korea's going to be a tough one to get on board because of their incredibly well-drilled armed forces and their dedication to their crazy leader. I considered leaving them alone, but I thought, *Why should I?* They don't have a divine right to make themselves exempt. They're not special. So they will be signing up. I don't wish to go into detail of how I will make that happen in case my letter gets intercepted in the post (if you are reading this as the interceptor, unlucky), but suffice it to say that I marvel at the wonder of just how much South Koreans look like North Koreans. How lucky we are that people with such similarities live right next door! What were the chances?! I will be using that really rather cleverly to our advantage. Expect a signature from Kim Jong-il in due course.

Finally, the Vatican. This one will not be a quick job. Six years ago, I had a plan. I applied to become the Pope. Under the strict rules of Catholicism, I qualify. Being both male and Catholic, I set about sending an application to take the role of the biggest and most influential religious leader on Earth. Yes, I am a Catholic man with religious values at my core. Yes, I wanted to improve the lives of a billion people worldwide with God as our guidance. Yes, I wanted to run my own country from a palace with a balcony view of the entire land. But my long-term vision was bigger.

Firstly, whilst owning a country is impressive for a religion, I wanted it to be bigger than that, so my first plan was to give up the country altogether but take over every other nation. Everyone who wasn't Catholic would move into Vatican City (which would probably be renamed to something less Catholic) whilst my lot could spread themselves about where they liked around the world. It was a way of encouraging more people to join what is the best faith on Earth.

But my main goal was actually to get us joined up with the IMF. I have always understood the importance of the IMF for global well-being, not just financially but for international relations, for countries to share and share alike without the disgusting drive for personal growth and power. These traits are vile and God does not like those people. That is why I am all about organising the world in what seem like radical ways, all for the greater good.

Unfortunately, I didn't get the job of Pope. They didn't even reply. To be honest, I left the bit about my plans to take over the rest of the world out of the letter because I wanted to retain my best bit for the interview. But it never came. I have now to decide whether to apply again in the future or hatch another plan to get them to sign up with us. I'm not really up for starting a religious war, though, so I might try and think of something else.

Mr. Lipsky, you are dumbfounded right now, I can sense it (even in the future, which for me is the case as I'm writing it, but you are not reading it as I am writing it, only in your time, which is not now as I'm writing). That's alright, that's OK. All I ask is that you speak to your people and invite me to come and give a short, two-day presentation on the plan I have outlined very basically in this first-stage application and also the many other ideas and practices I am going to implement upon my inauguration.

The IMF will become super-human under my super-gambling, super-powerful super-brain.

I look forward very much to meeting you and your colleagues at a convenient location very soon. Monaco?

Yours sincerely,

Sam Broadley

Capt. Sam Broadley

██████████

██████████

Ipswich

Suffolk

██████████

22nd July, 2011

Dear Sir Richard Branson,

I am writing to formally apply for the newly-created position of **Pilot** of your Virgin Galactic spaceship.

A quick word on yourself, which I know you'll appreciate: when I first heard your name linked with space travel, I thought, *Hang on – that bloke makes pickle. How can he go from inventing a tasty condiment to conquering space?* But then I felt silly because I realised you'd been making pickle for *years* and you moved on from that ages ago, big time, and the pickle thing is now a mere sideline. You went on to own the music industry and now you dominate the travel market.

My word, there really is no stopping you, is there, Sir, when it comes to travel? First trains, then planes, then balloons, now spacecraft. It looks to as if you're attempting to take over the universe as well as Earth! Good luck!

Anyway, this space travel malarkey – I like it, hence my application to be a part of it. Having researched your company (which I always do before approaching prospective employers), my understanding is that, at the present time, Virgin Galactic's technology currently allows (although no maiden voyage has taken place to date so you don't really know – I'm assuming that's why you're looking for a pilot) your craft to nip into space, maybe a few feet above the Earth, no more than the height of a tall man, and then fall back down (a controlled fall, of course, to prevent deaths).

I first thought this wasn't so impressive and what's the big deal because I've seen people go *way* into space even without a spacecraft, but then I remembered that was Superman and his foes and they're not real. So it turns out I *am* impressed. Bloody so. Obviously, people have been to the moon in the past, like Neil Armstrong, who was the first person to do so (which put whom I can only assume is his brother Louis to shame after he had sung a song about how wonderful the world is without even considering just how great the moon might be – Neil well and truly won that sibling rivalry!), but no-one's been there commercially. Until now. Well, shortly. Well, once we've done shorter journeys. Like the one I'll be piloting.

I have read a book of yours, Sir Richard (it was ever so good), which states that when you hire a pilot for one of your aeroplanes, a prerequisite is that he/she must have a minimum of ten years' experience of commercial flying. That is commendable and I thank you for ensuring the safety of loads of passengers who fly with you, of which I am not one. I think you only fly to the Americas and I've never been. Not because I don't like Americans. They're alright, for Americans.

At first, when I was considering whether I should be applying to be the pilot of your spaceship or not, I thought about your 'ten years' rule and thought I had little chance as my current practical flying time is zero hours in total. But then I realised: that rule was for *aircraft*. Not *spacecraft*. Unless you're looking for a man who's flown to the moon and back for the last ten years (which is unlikely – no-one's been there for bloody ages), that rule cannot apply. *I'm back on the horse!* I thought to myself. So here I am, writing this important letter to you, Sir. A letter that could change both our futures – almost certainly for the good.

You're probably wondering why you'd consider me at all if I have no spaceship-flying experience. OK, I'll tell you why you should. For a start, even though it's a load of boring nonsense to me, I've studied *Star Trek*, purely for its technical offerings as a way to progress my space exploration career. I'm feeling confident from that alone.

In addition, I play a lot of computer games that see me take the wheel of some star-searching space-vessel, guiding it through the galaxy, usually having to kill some devilish aliens along the way. Now, we don't know for certain if there is life elsewhere in the universe or not, but rest assured that if there is and we encounter aliens on our travels, you literally could not be safer than in my arms, Sir Rich. My experience of whacking the little buggers is second to none.

In case you're still not entirely confident, may I suggest that we conduct the interview within some kind of existing craft where I can just fly about a bit within Earth's boundaries? This will be simple for me compared to the undertaking of my space plans, and I'll easily be able to answer tough interrogating interview questions at the same time as negotiating our way through the Himalayan mountains or the tornadoes of Florida. I expect you'll offer me the job before we even land!

Before I accept the position, though, I'd like to ensure that our ambitions for the future of Virgin Galactic complement one another's. I'll have to listen to your side of things at the interview stage because it's only me writing this letter, but I'd like to outline my ideas now.

Whilst the current feat of leaving Earth by almost a couple of metres is indeed creditable (and it is – don't let anyone say any different), I am hoping that is the first, very quick step before moving on to bigger and better things. I'm expecting your rocket scientists to already be working on the next target, which must, in my opinion, be to conquer Jupiter. It's a *really* big place, which should make it less likely to miss the planet when I'm trying to land!

Also, if we can get there first, we can prepare for inevitable mass human migration by monopolising markets immediately with the likes of Virgin Space Hotels (which could be called Spotels), the development of vital Virgin Food (Spood) and Drinks (Spinks) as well as Virgin Space Trucks (Spucks). How exciting!

But not as exciting as going to Pluto. I wanna go there. It's a tiny planet, if indeed you can even call it a planet, it's so small. It's not a planet. Officially it might be, but it's more of a rock. A floating pebble. But it'd be nice to go there. The only problem is its commercial viability. I've heard it's so small you can only fit a handful of people on it. So that's me and some others. It's a long way to fly only a few individuals, but some people are mugs, like Elton John, and will pay anything just to be different, so I think it's doable. (I wonder if he'll sing *Rocket Man* to me as we travel…)

Ultimately, I have a huge ambition, which I would love to achieve with my favourite brand on the planet (and soon to be the universe): Virgin. I want to pilot the spacecraft that will travel so fast that myself and my special passengers will visit the end of the universe. I want to be able to see where it all started, how it started and, crucially, who started it. And I want *you* to be my front-seat passenger. In fact, I insist.

This can only be achieved by the out-of-the-box thinking of you, Sir

Richard of Virginshire, and your Virgin mega-brains, of whom I have great hope and expectations. I want this achieved bloody quickly so you need to get your men to work at the speed of light to get my spacecraft to *move at the speed of light and beyond.* Correct.

You can do it, my good man. You can *do* it. Marshall your men, rally your troops, lead your science-soldiers to create the ultimate rocket. Once you come good, I shall be ready and waiting in my astronauty gear (I've already got an outfit from the joke shop, but it'll probably need testing) to guide my super-rich and lucky passengers, who will have paid at least two-thirds of a billion pounds each to be on my ship, into the saucer before taking them – and you (for free) – on the trip of a lifetime. Hopefully it won't take a lifetime. In fact, if your boys do their jobs properly, we'll all come back younger than when we left. And we all want that.

So you can see that I'm not just a pilot, someone who's just basically a glorified bus driver, happy to move from A to B and B to A on repeat. I'm ambitious. I want to go beyond conventional imagination and see things no-one's dared even dream of.

I have motivated you, really excited you. I can tell. The adrenaline is overrunning the blood in your veins. The need to achieve is itching to release itself from your flesh. But if there's any part of you that ever doubts your need for me, Captain Sam Broadley, and my skills to fly you to universal glory, remember this:

I can ping your flying saucer anywhere you bloody well like.

I look forward to meeting you and dominating everything in the universe and possibly introducing you to God.

Yours sincerely,

Capt. Sam Broadley

PS: I'd like to call you Rick.

Sam Broadley

█████████

█████████

Ipswich

Suffolk

██████████

7th March, 2012

Dear Mr. David Bernstein,

I am writing to formally apply for the position of **England Manager**.

The first thing you will have seen in this letter is my name, assuming you read your correspondence in the conventional way from top to bottom. A reminder: (Mr.) Sam Broadley. Recognise it? You should. I applied back in 2000 after Kevin Keegan walked out. Actually, thinking about it, you might not have been on the panel at the time, but no doubt my name was bandied about the boardroom and beyond. If not, have a chat with old Adam Crozier – he'll tell ya.

Adam did reply to my written application. It detailed the criteria applicants ideally needed to cover and stated that a three-man shortlist had been drawn up. At no point did he say I wasn't on it so the obvious assumption was that I was. I was expecting the call imminently, requesting I head down to FA HQ quick-time to be interviewed.

That call never came. The next I heard was that Sven Goran Eriksson had been given the job. Worst of all, I had to hear about it through the media.

Was my mistreatment because Crozier was Scottish? Well, that's not for me to say. But in any case, I'm about as bitter as a strong lager, David, which isn't very bitter at all. I no longer feel resentment, I don't bear a grudge. I wasted many of the following years angry and confused, wondering what was so wrong with me, so repulsive that the FA cast me aside for a *foreigner*. But I decided long, long ago, back in the summer of 2010, that I must move on from this and accept that closure will never come my way.

Easier said than done, of course. But determination is one of my qualities and, bar the occasional sleepless night and odd breakdown, move on I did. I was comforted by the memories of several previous European and World Cup campaign failures, first by Swedish Sven, followed by Steve "Wally-With-a-Brolly, Paint-My-Smile-On" McClaren and finally Fabio Capello, the Italian who spoke fewer words of English than a deaf mute but slightly more than Wayne Rooney.

The debacle of Capello's reign ends (one hopes) a period in time when foreign flavours painted a poisonous paste on the palate of English football. No longer (one prays) will we have to accept a fellow from beyond our shores to be the one to lead our men. Never again (one begs) must we watch a passionless non-patriot walk the touchline of Wembley pretending he a) knows what he's doing and b) cares.

The time has come for you to bring in a man who not only has bundles of talent, knowledge, leadership and class but, crucially, has the burn of pure English desire.

This is where I, a Lion with a roar to crush the confidence of even the hardest of Germans, will finally come in.

I spoke in my previous application of my success as a manager. In case my letter is no longer on file, I will briefly outline my credentials.

A left-footed defender or creative midfielder or forward (equally impressive in any), I was a bloody good player in my day. But I let the world down by not coming to fruition. That was my fault. Food was more important to me (and some would argue rightly so as food is one of the two basic things that keeps one alive – at the risk of sounding like a girl, football is just a game; priorities). Having failed to reach professional standard, I turned my hand to management, first with my local Under-7s side. Two consecutive seasons finishing fourth proved my consistent top-level capability.

I realised I was destined for bigger things and applied for England Manager. Unexpected failure led me to take on a new challenge as I took on a coaching role with a load of Under-14s. They were ill-disciplined yobs, quite frankly, and useless at football, but I soon asserted my authority and turned them into basic players and survived apparent certain relegation. This nailed on further top-class skills in my managerial armour: man-management and a winning mentality. It's fair to say I was fast becoming hot property.

In 2004, I took on a player/coach role for Lenton Griffins FC, a team that created the Guinness World Record for the Longest Ever Football Tour. We played 15 matches across Europe and Africa, and it was vital we equipped ourselves with style and guile while representing our country. My proven coaching skills were put firmly to the test, and by way of leading by example on the pitch, I led us to two wins, three draws and just ten defeats (one being a well-fought 21-0 reverse against Raja Casablanca, the African Champions' League Winners). Quite an impressive record, I think you'll agree. We got on Sky Sports News and everything! And subsequently, another remarkable box ticked on my CV: international experience under the international spotlight.

Mr. Bernstein, I've made my feelings clear on the matter of my application back in 2000. I've told you how much the treatment of me by the FA hurt and the time it took me to move on. But I've showed you how I did overcome the personal mental torture by working on my management game whilst, crucially I feel, continuing to *play* the game. I look back now at my first approach to the FA and my denial of an interview and can understand their take on it, probably seeing the step from Martlesham Youth Under-7s to England Coach as more of a sizeable leap. I maintain that I could have made that leap, but football is, as they say, a matter of opinions.

I have waited a few weeks since Capello's exit before writing to you in the hope you may have approached me. That has obviously yet to happen (unless I receive a letter in the time it takes for this one to arrive on your desk, in which case, I accept). The stand-off has reminded me very much of my early school discos where the boys were on one side of the room and girls on the other, neither daring to make the first move. Well, I've decided to grow a pair and make that move for the sake of the nation.

Stuart Pearce took a friendly against Holland recently and lost. That should put him immediately out of the frame. Glenn Hoddle has said he wants it but he's already had a go so that's not fair. Harry Redknapp, the people's favourite (the people don't know me yet (probably)), is sitting on the fence, saying how much he loves Spurs. Well, if he loves them that much, he can bloody stay there. My point is this: even if I'm *not* number one on your shortlist, by default, I'm your man. I think you can see that now.

When you appoint me, I want you to know that there will be no delay my end in me starting the job should you want me immediately. I work for Suffolk Police and am supposed to give four weeks' notice, but I'm more than happy to let them down and walk. Most of 'em support England so they shouldn't get too upset when they see I'm doing it for Queen and country.

By the way, we all know of the debacle when Rooney got himself sent off in the last qualifying game and he's now out of the first two games of the Euro Finals. And we also recently learned that Darren Bent, our number two striker, is likely to be out through injury. Well, I didn't really want to do this, but I've begun training again with a view to probably playing myself up front, possibly alongside Theo Walcott. I'm more of a target man than out-and-out striker and I'm more than good enough to feed Theo and his pace. In fact, I'm so good that I won't just feed him, I'll chew it up for him as well. Please don't think this is me playing the power card because it's not. I know I'm probably not as good as Rooney so providing I haven't set the Finals alight (which isn't necessarily unlikely), he will be drafted straight back into the team after his suspension and I'll take my rightful place on the bench.

In any case, now we're agreed I'm the man, I look forward very much to receiving a reply and the prospect of taking on our country's great football team and leading us to immediate glory (or later if you want some other muppet to lead us in the Euros first).

Yours sincerely,

Sam "The Gaffer" Broadley

PS: For a more detailed look at my history, please find enclosed my footballing CV. (I challenge you to *not* get excited by it!)

PPS: I've gone to the trouble of already 'going the extra mile' in my new job by writing a European Football Championships team song. I'm dabbling with the idea of releasing it and 25% of the proceeds going to charity. The players will of course be singing it (as backing vocalists and cameos while I perform the main lyrics). I don't want to spoil the surprise but to give you a taste, it starts with:

Johnny Terry is an arse, is an arse, is an arse.

More from me later!

SAM BROADLEY'S SUPER SOCCER CV

- **1980, aged 0 (unborn):** Kicked my mum in the womb.

- **1985, aged 4:** Kicked my mum on the shin. Reprimanded (second offence).

- **1986, aged 5:** Watched my first televised football match. I can't remember it.

- **1987, aged 6:** Began playing matches in school at playtime. Last pick. Always. Or not at all.

- **1988, aged 7:** Won my first tackle, scored my first goal. I told Teacher. Confidence grew.

- **1989, aged 8:** Joined local village team, Martlesham Youth. Shone. Summer tournament winner on debut. Deserved (overdue) respect finally being earned.

- **1993, aged 12:** Picked for Suffolk County team. True.

- **1994, aged 13:** Trial with Cambridge United School of Excellence (now Academy). Failed. Manager made poor decision. Look where they are now.

- **1995, aged 14:** Trial with Ipswich Town School of Excellence (again, now Academy). Success. Manager made excellent decision.

- **1996, aged 15:** Missed open goal (not even a goalkeeper) against Peterborough United in front of First Team Manager, George Burley. Unimpressed.

Later made up for the embarrassment by nutmegging Keiron Dyer in training whilst hopping. Everyone laughed. A lot. Respect retrieved.

- **1997, aged 16:** Released by Ipswich Town. Poor decision, which I think they regret to this day. Not as much as me, mind.

  Went into management – Martlesham Youth Under-7s. Three seasons, two competitive. Finished fourth in each. Brilliant achievement (if you saw 'em).

- **2000, aged 19:** Joined University of Lincoln and respective football club Third Team. AKA the Poor Team. Camaraderie high, skill low, victories few. Not my fault.

  Applied for England Manager's job. Failed. Devastated.

- **2001/02, aged 20/21:** Rightly promoted to First Team. Manager's Player of the Year. A good decision. Didn't win Players' Player. Only one person voted for me: the Manager.

- **2002-2006, aged 22-25:** Various amateur appearances. More for them than me (big name).

- **2003, aged 22:** Headhunted to coach my mate's failing Under-14s team. Tasked with survival. Achieved. Celebrated (me by them).

- **2004, aged 23:** Became Guinness World Record holder for being in the team that achieved the Longest Ever Football Tour. Scored 40-yard (average distance taken from various estimates) equaliser in a 3-3 draw at the Millennium Stadium.

- **2006, aged 25:** Newfound desire to reach the top thwarted by a serious knee injury. Out of the game in all capacities (playing and coaching) until 2009.

- **2008, aged 27:** Travelled to 138 football stadiums across Britain by minibus in under 138 hours in the name of charity. Now very good at getting to matches.

- **2009, aged 28:** Widely-anticipated comeback in tour of India. Injured in first five minutes of opening match. Out of tour. Went on to get food poisoning.

- **2011, aged 30:** Headhunted again (by same mate as before) to save local Under-10s side. Progress made but left due to undisclosed personal reasons.

  Another playing comeback (seven-a-side) – one-game tour of Europe. Best player in a 9-7 victory in Turkey. Did not win Man of the Match award. Widely-accepted footballing travesty.

- **2012, aged 31:** Applied for Manager of England. Await acceptance. Press conference unveiling speech already written.

13th April, 2012

Dear Mr. Broadley,

Thank you for your recent letter regarding the England Manager's job.

As I'm sure you can appreciate, we have received a large number of queries of this nature since the recent announcement.

We would like to thank you for taking the time to get in touch. Please keep an eye on our website for the latest news on this topic – www.thefa.com.

Thank you again for getting in touch.

Yours sincerely,

Customer Relations

Sam Broadley

Ipswich
Suffolk

25th July, 2012

Dear Archbishop Dr. Williams,

I am writing to formally apply for the position of **Archbishop of Canterbury** once you have vacated, as announced some time ago.

I've been an ardent follower of yours, Doctor, for a number of years, and will continue to be so. Well, depending on what you're doing next; if it's anything Satanic, then obviously I'll cease.

I've written to your fine self because having researched the 'official' route in which to apply, I see that it's riddled with bureaucracy and farce. First, the Prime Minister has to select a selection committee! Then the committee have to select their recommendation! Then it has to be taken to the Queen! What a farce. So I come to you directly in an attempt to woo you by my application and ask you to cut out all the nonsense and make the recommendation yourself.

And with the godlike goodness I can bring to the world, you will know I am that man.

Currently, the system is too slow to hire, to the point of, in my opinion, being immoral. I don't think God would be too happy. He built us to move, to make things happen, not chat. If He wanted us to gabble, He wouldn't have given us full bodies, just mouths. For this reason, despite being a Catholic, I have made the move to act under the command of God Himself to get this letter written. In the word of Steven Spielberg: *ACTION!*

I say under God's command but I don't mean that literally. That is, He didn't appear in front of me and say, "Sam, will you *please* just go and apply for that bloody Archbishop job like you should've done weeks ago, you fool." I mean I felt it in my *heart* that I think I should try to please Him. You get these people who say they've spoken to God. You get *loads* of those people. Yeah, well, anyone can speak to God... it's when you're chatting with Him face-to-face I wanna hear about it.

The fact is no-one knows where He is. Despite being ready to take on the role of Head of the State Church, even *I* cannot tell you *where* He is. So *if* we don't know where He is, how can we say if He is. We can't. And we shouldn't assume that He exists. He does of course... *in our hearts,* in some form or other. Hence the reason I heard the message in my *heart*. Hence this letter in your *hand(s)* (unless it is resting on a table).

So what can I offer the role of Archbishop? Well, I'm a raving religious rebel, for one. By raving, I don't mean lunatic, nor homosexual, and I'm not into raves, although I enjoy a spot of clubbing, but not of seals. I'm actually quite level-headed.

By religious, I mean I'm quite religious. I've always been a big fan of God. As a self-made Man, He wasn't afraid to get His hands dirty. He's done some fine work, especially when He later evolved it into a family business.

By rebel, I mean I'm rebellious. By rebellious, I don't mean in the traditional yobbish way, you know, ignoring curfews, getting grounded for answering back, giving the 'V' to the law-makers, playing rock music, throwing hard-boiled eggs at teachers' faces, drawing phallic symbols on the youth club wall... I've not done those things for literally *years*. I'm 31 now so, despite the odd recent slip-up, I'm way too mature to be getting mixed up in all that nonsense.

What I mean is that I have the type of attitude that doesn't *conform to the norm*. I pour scorn upon the boring in life. The stagnant. The stale. The monotonous. The soulless. Anything that makes me yawn. But the Church of England isn't all bad, it just needs shaking up.

Let's face it: it lacks sex appeal. You might ask how it could *ever* possibly have it after some bloke once sat down and wrote a little book called *The Bible* and penned the words, 'quoting' God Himself,

> *"Though shalt not talk of nor celebrate nor displayeth nor expresseth anything to do with sex thereof…especially in My House and My Garden… and, thereby, never should Man and Woman enjoyeth such an act nor even chat about it joyethly or otherwise…"*

Or something like that, I can't quite remember the exact words. It's been a while since I sat down with the Good Book but I think it's somewhere near the middle. In fact, I should be able to find the page because I remember squashing a fly on that particular leaf as it was getting right on my nerves. But the point is that the Church is grey and dull. It's unappealing to new people. Yes, you might get plenty of kids born into the Church of England, but it's in name only. They'd much rather know what colour knickers Britney's wearing (if any).

We live in a sexually liberal society these days. Right or wrong, that's a fact. (I for one think it's right, but that's 'cause I luuurve the chicks!) In this celebrity-obsessed culture we find ourselves in, do you continue to fight an unwinnable fight to desperately maintain non-promiscuous behaviour or do you get on board, get your kit off and jump around together in jelly?! It's a no-brainer, really. Jelly tastes good. And it *feels* good upon your glorious, God-given skin.

I *really* want to be Archbishop, and if (when) I get this gig, the thing I most want to do is bring it into the modern world. How? By affiliating ourselves with the sexy celebrities. Out goes the Good Book, in comes Kelly Brook!

I use Brook as an example just because it rhymes with Book. Dunno if you noticed that. Just one of my witticisms (surely a prerequisite…?). But I don't necessarily mean her. We actually need to get a whole party of celebs in, anyone who is current, sexy and, ideally, slightly unruly. I'm thinking Robbie Williams and Jessie J: one's a sex-addict and former druggie, the other's a half-lesbian. I'm speaking respectively.

Currently, we've got Prince Charles heading up the religion. He may be described as a lot of things, but 'hot' is not one of them. His missus even less so. Is that gonna boost our numbers? No need to answer; it's rhetorical. So to the back go the royals, up step the celebs. But what do we do with them? How will they help promote the Church?

My idea is simple. Gather as many of these celebs together as possible. Once rounded up, we are going to act out a new version of *The Bible*. It won't be an overhaul, just… contemporised. Sexed up, if you will. We'll capture on camera a full and modern adaptation of the entire story and air it to our public in all good cinemas. And bad ones if necessary.

For example, for *'In the Beginning…'*, I will recruit Boris Johnson and Nigella Lawson to play Adam and Eve. As a slight twist, instead of Adam persuading Eve to eat the forbidden apple, he ends up getting her to munch on a massive banana. So not too different but enough to make it exciting. And this-shaped food was *definitely* outlawed by God in the early days of the world.

But in our new version of the Good Book, we see that God becomes more liberal as the years pass, and as He chills out, we watch the number of people increase dramatically while our happy celebs fornicate with joy right across the Big Man's garden.

I have yet to cast God in my mind. By the time it comes to filming, I will be a celebrity myself having been the Archbishop for a while so could quite naturally play Him, but really I see our Lord being perfectly portrayed by Dizzee Rascal.

It might seem ludicrous to do what I'm suggesting, but it's high time we brought the Church into the 21st century. Without my intervention, the Church will, as generations pass, decline uncontrollably until it is but a metaphorical, and possibly literal, ruin.

You'll have noticed I mentioned I'm a Catholic. That probably doesn't help my cause, I know, but there are two things you should consider. First off, I am willing to change allegiance to get the job. I have no morals whatsoever. From your perspective, that's getting one over the rival so should interest you. Secondly, I will at some point during my reign be looking to form a merger with the Catholics, which isn't all that radical because we were all as one once upon a time. Both clubs were ruled by the Pope. I must admit now that *that* is the job I *really* want. But because of my newfound love for the Church of England, I'm only going to be Pope if I can own both. You should and, no doubt, will love me for that.

Please forward me as your recommendation at your earliest

convenience. It's important we act soon after too many weeks of *in*action. I can feel my flock getting restless.

Yours sincerely,

Mr. Sam Broadley

Sam Broadley

Ipswich
Suffolk
ENGLAND

28th February, 2013

Dear Cardinal (the one that opens this letter),

I am writing to formally apply for the available position of **Pope**.

So this gig has become available since our old friend Benedict XVI upped sticks and left. It was a surprise, to say the least, but I was not surprised. He was a controversial appointment in the first place, what with his German roots and all, and I think he knew this even then and wanted to exit pre-death as a final mark of rebellion.

Good on him, I say. I mean, the first Pope to slip off the robes (publicly) in 600 years is a big deal, but he gets to see his successor in action, unlike the previous few. Hitler didn't give himself that opportunity.

Although he can watch from afar as the next man steps into his oh-so-big red shoes as he wallows in the glory of a 40-nun swimming pool-party retirement, he will no doubt be hoping the new kid on the block fails.

I can't blame him for this. I've never wanted to be outdone and outperformed when someone has taken My job upon My departure, forced or otherwise, even on the rare occasions when I've loved the organisation I've left (as Bene presumably does his…). I've wanted it to continue to thrive but in no way at all thanks to the job vulture who'd jumped in for My scraps. In fact, in an ideal world, I've wanted him to be entirely detrimental to the cause.

And this is how Mr. Ratzinger (or Ratface as he's affectionately known to some of his loving followers) is feeling right now as he prepares to watch the newbie take the reins.

Well, my faith-loving friend, it is down to you and all your cassock-donning Cardinal colleagues to ensure that our next pontiff is far and beyond better than our abandoning *freund* to make sure that he lives to regret his decision to give up control of 1.2 billion worshipers.

This is where I, a colossal Catholic, too colossal for Cardinal, come in.

Too colossal for Cardinal, I say. Said because I am not a cardinal, nor do I have a wish to be, nor is there a desire from God for Me to be. Not because I am not worthy… the *job* is not worthy of *Me*. It is beneath Me.

Gosh, that sounds arrogant. Please don't take it as such. These are not My words. They were spoken to Me by God Himself. Let Me tell you when. This'll make you laugh!

When I was 16, I played the role of Jesus in a high school production of *Jesus Christ: Superstar*. Was I in fact a superstar? Not for Me to say, nor would I, despite what I think and know. But I was certainly Jesus Christ. Not *the* Jesus, obviously; He now lives in our hearts. But I was somewhere close to actually *being* He. I just knew it.

At first, I wondered if I just felt like I was because of My incredible acting ability whereby I can lose Myself in a character, *become* them, make My audience believe I am *actually* them. But as I went through My pre-show prayers in the canteen before the closing show, praying for yet another outstanding portrayal of *God's Son, God's voice actually appeared before Me.*

I couldn't specifically *see* it; it was oral and aural. But it was as though I could see it such was the clarity. Despite the incredible warmth I felt in My heart at that moment, I told Myself it must just be heartburn from the rock cake I had consumed earlier in that very room.

But the voice spoke to Me clearly as though in that canteen with Me, at the serving hatch. It said to Me, "SAAAAAMMM. YOU *ARE* MY SOOOONNN."

As I heard those words, I jumped over the counter to check it wasn't my mate Ross, who was playing Judas, playing a prank by speaking through a megaphone. I knew the school had one. "Piss off, Ross!" I tested. But no reply. Only silence. I immediately regretted swearing in the likely presence of God. As I scanned the darkened room, I caught a glimpse of a massive, thick leg with an extra-large sandal attached follow an inhumanly big, robed back of a person exit a window.

I knew this was God Himself. I raced to the window in the hope of catching a further peep, and I'm sure I saw Him run off towards the caretaker's house and out of sight. I considered running after Him, asking Him why He spoke to Me. *Why Me?* I wanted to know. *Why am I afforded such special treatment in the form of a personal visit? Why am I Your Son?*

But I couldn't do it. He was off to see the caretaker for a reason. Terry was the caretaker. Maybe he had been chosen, too, although he didn't seem special enough to Me. He wasn't about to portray

---

the Lord's Son in a hit high school musical show. He just swept floors and cleared gutters. But Terry was a good man. He was exceptionally thick-set, and I always remember he seemed to wear a long white jacket and summer footwear, regardless of the time of year and entirely ignorant of the fashion of the time. He liked a joke, too. Always playing pranks on pupils, was Terry!

But it was this encounter with our maker that changed My life forever. I now knew what My purpose in life was – to spread the word of Him and protect His people. So I went on stage, became Jesus (to the point where apparently some people in the audience were convinced it was the Second Coming) and later mulled over how to best serve God.

The trouble was that I didn't know how to do it, even as Jesus's Brother, which is how I now considered Myself. Weeks rolled on. Then months and then years. I was lost. I needed God to tell Me what to do but He was proving to be a stay-away dad and I began to resent Him for it.

As I struggled along alone, I considered all kinds of things. My best idea, and one I kind of regret not going with, was to become a vigilante. There is so much suffering in our world, I wondered if I could rid it all for God and His people by systematically wiping the bad from Earth, seeing off scum like the chavs on the estate near mine. I didn't, though. Honestly. There's just too many of 'em so it didn't seem worth starting.

But it was only when Pope Benedict stepped aside did I realise what My calling was: to be Pope. *That's* what God wants Me to do. I mean, I did apply for this job back in 2005, but I thought I was the only one who wanted me to have it, not God as well. How wrong I was. So now you know God wants Me to be Pope and you know *I* want to be Pope, you really ought to seriously consider that I should be Pope. You may go to Hell if you don't.

Cardinal, should the above anecdote and endorsement from God Himself not be enough to convince you and your friends, please know some of the things I will do for us all and for the Catholic Church. I will talk to you in detail when we meet about everything I want to happen and instigate, but for now I wish to talk of just one of My ideas because I feel this could be the single thing that brings forth peace among our peoples across the world.

For reasons beyond My comprehension, the varying religions just aren't getting along. No matter what we try, all the others think they're right. *Even* the Scientologists! Now obviously, we know we're right, but *we've* got to respect the views of all the others who believe in their stuff. We're already pretty tolerant, but not all of them are. I know it's childish, but it's a fact. So what do we do?

My proposal is to organise an inter-religious football World Cup. We'll host the inaugural event at the Vatican to ensure we qualify, but the rest will have to go through a qualifying process. We will expect the bigger religions to bring stronger teams to the competition as they will have many more people in the pool to choose from, so I'm expecting it to come down to probably semi-finals between ourselves, the Protestants, the Jews and the Muslims. There is the chance, of course, that a couple of minnows, like the Mormons or Jedi Knights, might cause a huge upset and knock one of the big guns out.

I am exceptionally competitive and I want to win. I will be the Pope, but that does not make Me too big to play. I am good enough to star and so I shall, let that be known now. You lot are too old, but I can get down with the kids such are My excellent communication skills, so I will find the best footballers the Catholic world can offer.

Although hooliganism is known in the world of football, I strongly believe that, with the right marketing, we can bring all religions together through the worldwide language of soccer. Then we'll get them all to convert.

Please consider My words so very carefully. The above action is just one idea to ensure the world comes together as one, to gain everyone's trust and then watch as they all realise that we were right all along and there will be one worldly religion, of which I will be leader. Forever.

My friends, THAT is My calling. THAT is what God asked Me to do in His name. And then in *My* name once He retires. It's no lie to say:

I EXPECT TO BECOME GOD.

I so look forward to meeting you all in person and thrashing out My ideas to you in order for you to realise that I am The One to guide you to the Promised Land.

Yours sincerely,

Mr. Sam Broadley (God-to-be)

Sam Broadley

██████████

██████████

Ipswich

Suffolk

████████

24th July, 2013

Dear BBC,

I am writing to formally apply for the role of **Doctor Who** on *Doctor Who*.

I was absolutely delighted when the news broke that Matt Smith was leaving the role. He wasn't the most impressive Doctor ever, I think we can agree. I'd quite liked to have seen him killed off, in actual fact, but that cannot be, for it would've meant the end of Doctor Who.

Instead, regeneration, as it is known, is required for me to take on the esteemed position as the biggest saviour of mankind to exist since the birth of Jesus (although not even Him really, not through any fault of His own; He was a very good man, but the arguments and carnage in His name ever since His great work, dear me, quite the sad irony...).

So anyway, the show has enjoyed a resurgence since 2005 after a sixteen-year absence. Initially aimed at children back in the '60s, it quickly won a following of all ages, particularly down to its gory content, the broadcast of which brought complaints aplenty from mums, citing it as violence of unprecedented proportions. Well, actually, it was preceded by incredibly *real* violence only *one day* before the Time Lord's first ever public appearance... the well-televised assassination of President John F. Kennedy of the United States of America.

Now, I'm not saying that particular murder had an influence on the writers of *Doctor Who*. If anything, it actually upstaged the Doctor's first outing. That must have been annoying. But the BBC should've used the incredibly violent JFK wipe-out to assassinate idiots' claims that the apparently brutal war between the Time Lord and the Daleks was, in comparison, nothing but a tickle-tussle in the TARDIS. (I'm fully aware the TARDIS was for transportation only and no fighting took place within; I just wrote it for alliterative purposes.) (Is it correct, by the way, that TARDIS stands for 'Time Lord's Aroma Ruins Daleks Into Submission'? I was once told that. I still have no idea what it stands for if not.)

If you look back now at old episodes, the so-called violence is laughable, really bloody laughable. Actually, the *lack* of violence is something that puts me off the old episodes. And the more recent ones. *And* the new ones, to be perfectly honest with you. The absence of brute force, blood, guts, burning of flesh, stabbings and proper fist-fighting really makes me angry. It's a good job I can hold my temper else I might punch the BBC right in the face.

My view, which is often the right one, is that family programmes should always contain an element of hardcore violence. Maybe 40-45% of any given episode. You hear some 'educated' sorts talk of sex and violence on telly nurturing children into killers and whatnot. What a load of nonsensical nonsense. Perfect counter-argument: There's a band called *The Killers* – does that mean a child will start brandishing a gun at innocent passers-by when they listen to their *Best Of* album? Of course bloody not.

Violence is a necessary part of our every-day world. People achieved *nothing* over the millennia without physically ruining people. That is why war remains as popular now as it ever has been. It's like sport but more fruitful. Instead of hiding children from the real world and all its glorious violence, let them embrace and enjoy it. A good parent prepares their young for the big, wide world, for the day they flee the nest to fend for themselves. Let them watch and be violent to their hearts' content in order to become a true success in life.

Now I've proven to you that violence is everything, I am sure you will embrace it yourselves for the next series of *Doctor Who* (if colleagues disagree, make sure you physically tell them you're right). I know, love and understand violence, but what else can I offer the role? What experience do I have?

Well, I'm not a doctor, I'll tell you that right away. I know an application letter is about selling oneself and displaying one's credentials, but I'm honest and it's best you know now than find out later and we've all wasted our time. I'm probably intelligent enough to be a doctor, I just have no interest in saving lives. I currently work for the police. I don't even like doing that really because it means helping people, but it pays the bills.

I have done loads of entertaining for people, though. I don't mind doing that. I believe one should always make a difference to people's lives in any way they can. It's just the morally right thing to do. My experience is mainly on stage in various shows, making people laugh with my (scripted-by-other-people) memoirs and musings. I've also done some live television work (I was on a quiz show back in 2004; the show itself was a flop but I was brilliant, except I didn't win a penny, a fact I have yet to get over) so working the cameras will not be a problem to me.

I've yet to become a lord, a disappointment in my life to date, particularly as I am definitely worthy of such a title. The closest I have ever got to being a proper lord is when I was a gaylord. I wasn't *actually* a gaylord, not in the least, it's just what the lads used to call me growing up. I mean, there was no real evidence I was gay. I loved girls, bloody so. I'd rarely even touch a boy; it just wasn't for me, despite his efforts. I'm not *anti*-gay, you know. I've got loads of gay friends. They seem to love me a bit *too* much, though, and I'm a bit of a flirt, but I'd never want to get sexual, even if a couple of them *are* very handsome. I'm regretting this paragraph. I could delete it and then you'd never see it. But I won't. I'm an idiot. But not a gaylord one.

Anyway, to sum up, I want to be your next Doctor Who and so do you (you want *me* to be, not you want *you* to be). Or you will do once you've met me, of that I can assure you. I love *Doctor Who* (although he's not my favourite; my favourite is Doctor Schurr who is based locally; he was ever so good to me when I hurt my heel) and I resolutely believe that I am the best man to take this staple of British society forward to appeal to further and wider audiences and vastly improve the violence of children across the globe to massively accelerate the progress of Mankind.

DON'T BE A GAYLORD – MAKE ME YOUR TIME LORD.

(Please don't consider that last sentence to be homophobic; I was simply making a light-hearted reference to the earlier paragraph on the subject of gaylording, one which I am still regretting.)

I look forward to receiving your response in the near future. Don't make me jump in the TARDIS to go get it. (Now *that's* a better reference!)

Yours sincerely,

(To-be) Doctor Who
WHOOOOO??? Doctor Sam D. Broadley, that's who!!!

Sam Broadley

Ipswich
Suffolk

1st October, 2013

Dear Mr. Jeremy Hunt MP,

I am writing to you, Jeremy, as the Health Secretary, to formally apply for the available position of **Chief** of the NHS.

A quick fact: 'NHS' stands for National Health System. I'm sure you already know that, but sometimes, when one uses acronyms for as long as one does, one can soon forget what they stand for! So that was for you, just in case. I also wanted to prove that I have done my research in preparation for this application. Now proven, I can move on to the next stage.

The next stage being the expression of my love for and devotion to the National Health System (which I will refer to as the NHS from now on for fear of looking like a bragger, continually showing off my obvious knowledge). I really love it and I'm really devoted to it.

A quick twenty-two words on my eventual predecessor, Sir David Nicholson: He seemed to do an OK job under great pressure, a tenure during which he was let down by many beneath him. It would be unfair to delve any deeper into his time at the helm. I would, and, I'm sure, so would you, prefer to look forward to the next man to take charge of the stethoscope and guide our nation's health to a hearty future.

When the NHS was formed back in 1948 (my knowledge on this

subject astounds even me sometimes), it was set to become one of the bedrocks of our society, envied by the world over. I sometimes sit back and really think about this service, I mean *really* think about it, how incredible it is that this country is good enough to provide *free healthcare* to each and every man, woman and child in the UK (United Kingdom (brilliant)).

Occasionally, I find myself driving to a nearby hospital and just sitting outside, watching, watching as people hobble about, get wheeled in and out, ambulances (ambulae?) screeching here, there and everywhere. Sometimes, I wander about the corridors, staring at the injured and incapable filling up the waiting areas. I peer into examination rooms and operating theatres, spying the derobed and exposed, admiring their willingness for a man in a white jacket to prod, poke and probe at his leisurely leisure. It very much makes me want to be a doctor.

I shake my head in wonderment as I think to myself, *They're getting all this for free! FREE!!* But I did learn from my recent research that we are all actually *paying* for it indirectly through *taxes*! I always wondered what the Government was taking money off me for, and now I know, it makes me want to get my money's worth because I don't get operated on nearly enough.

I think, though, to cause myself injury just to get into hospital is a bit risky. I've heard stories about people not surviving hospital treatment, and I've got too much to offer the world to suffer that fate, particularly if it's self-inflicted. So the more likely option is to quit work so the Government can take money from me no longer. That way, I won't be able to afford to eat and so will probably get ill and hospitalised and my treatment really will be for free! I'm so clever.

Thinking about it, though, I'm a workaholic so I don't want to give up. In fact, I've just reminded myself that this is an application letter for a job, which tells me that I really do want to work. Of that, there is no doubt. Actually, when I become the Chief of the NHS, I will in effect be *paid* for any future treatment thanks to my huge salary *from* the NHS! This gig sounds better and better. Please note my smart and creative brainpower when considering my application.

So with the post of NHS Chief due to be up for grabs upon the retirement of Nicholson in March next year, you really need to be thinking about who is going to be taking over. There have been no announcements since the news broke of Dave's forthcoming exit so presumably you're in a quandary and don't know where to turn.

This is where I, a health have-a-go hero, come in.

Yes, because I will have a bloody good go at being a hero and return ill people's good health to them on mass. But don't take that at face value – read about it next.

There are a number of ways in which I will improve service levels of the NHS to levels never before seen. I will reduce spending, bureaucracy, management, patient waiting times and nurses. But how? Well, in the incorrectly pluralised word of some meerkat on telly – simples:

I will authorise patients to mend each other.

By which I mean that, in order to reduce waiting times for regular, every-day injuries, illnesses and disorders, waiting rooms will be stocked up with all the necessary equipment and drugs to enable those waiting to see a nurse or doctor to actually sort each other out.

So to take a hypothetical example, a man called Kevin comes rushing into A&E (Accident & Emergency (I really am good)) with a nasty cut to his neck caused by, say, a furious wild animal. Let's say a meerkat as they've already had a mention. An initial check by a secretary on the front desk shows that the menacing meerkat did not manage to get to the jugular, as was its likely intention (you just have to look at their vicious faces to realise that), and it is, therefore, not deemed to be life-threatening and so is a non-emergency.

Meanwhile, a woman stumbles through the A&E doors having a panic attack, legs and arms flailing about everywhere. Let's call her Mary. She's in obvious distress and needs help. The now-highly trained secretary is able to make a judgement call that there is no requirement for a doctor or nurse to deal. So in line with new protocol, she summons Kevin to take charge of her. Whilst clutching his neck, Kevin consults the appropriate leaflet found behind the seating area in the 'Leaflets' section and knows immediately to jump on Mary to control her erratic limbs, taking care to not take a wayward toe to the jugular.

Once her arms and legs are tied with gaffer tape, as per the leaflet, he will then apply the brown paper bag for her breathing, inject the Valium and thus successfully cure the woman. Once she's entirely calm, she will then meticulously apply some codeine to our Kevin's wound and stich him up. We then have two mended patients – all without even a peek of a doctor!

I am so excited by this plan. Think of the money it will save. Think of the time it will free up for doctors and nurses to provide care to the seriously ill. Think of the hugely-reduced waiting times. Think of the surplus nurses we can totally get rid of. Think of the community spirit it will bring, the boom in love among total strangers. It can *only* be a winner.

While I'm romanticising about Kevin and Mary's plight, I envisage them falling for each other romantically. It will be a bit like the wartime stories of love where soldiers and local fair maidens would entwine themselves with one another in the midst of terrible times. Neither Kevin nor Mary will have wished to find themselves within the confines of a hospital, but as they go out of the doors hand in hand, they will have been so grateful for such an act of fate in the form of an attack by a vile animal and a mental turn occurring simultaneously at a given moment in time. One could not fail to realise that it was meant to be…

So turning a hospital into a dual community mending place-slash-dating agency can only be a good thing. I expect it to go on to big things and be replicated around the world. Never again will a sick man be without a spouse.

This is just one of thousands of ideas I will be implementing when you sign me up for this job. All I'm asking for in return is a massive salary, an equally stupendous pension that I can draw at any time and free access to a local gym. Don't worry about healthcare; I'll already have that on tap (and I'll be *paid* for it!!!)

Read: you need me. The NHS's reputation needs to be saved – and I am its saviour. From Day One, I will inject a huge dose of sense into this otherwise poisonous and pus-filled cyst of a service. I will perform a full and frank scan of the system, dissecting and analysing samples from a host of bodies within. Through hard (skin-)graft, I will probe away up top and down below. There will be no anaesthetic applied while I perform a multiple bypass of all its terrible operations. No pain, no gain. But with the resulting upheaval and turmoil such an intrusion will induce, I will be personally nursing the National Health System back to its once vibrant self.

Friend, I hold the ultimate prescription. Let me be your life-saving medicine. Your saviour.

I look forward to hearing from you in due course with a view to becoming the life-saver and love-giver of everybody everywhere.

Yours sincerely,

Mr. Sam D. Broadley

Sam Broadley

█████████████

Ipswich

Suffolk

████████

17th November, 2015

Dear Mr. Ian Ritchie,

I am writing to formally apply for the currently available position of **Head Coach** of the England rugby team.

My aim is to type this letter to you as quickly as I possibly can because, if press reports are to be believed (and we know they always are), it is looking like you are going to be making a swift appointment. I am having to get in there quickly, quicker than George North flying past his woeful English counterparts.

I ought to point out here that my natural tendency when writing letters of application is to take my time, deliberate, methodically choose my wording and phraseology to educate the lucky recipient and furnish him or her with the facts to prove I am a great man (a job application is no place to be humble) who can have the greatest of impacts upon the respective role for which I am applying. So to now be typing like a madman flies in the face of my normal course, but if nothing else, it will prove to you that no matter the pressure, I can adapt to change, respond to sudden variants and act rapidly and impressively.

It may sound, at this point, that I apply for a lot of jobs. I want to reassure you that I most certainly do not, Mr. R. I am exceptionally selective. I will only go for those roles that I am entirely suited to take on, where I can make a very real difference and bring positive change to the organisation, country and, if at all possible, the world as a whole. That is why I so desire to be the main man in English rugby. *That* surely reassures you sufficiently to read on with anticipation and excitement as you seek to learn all about my greatness.

You see, I sit here in a seat at my local library (I had to get away from the missus and kid – you know what it's like, always being given jobs and no time for yourself to change the world) typing my fingertips off for your benefit, Ian: to stop you, as the Chief Executive of the RFU, making a rash decision – for the sake of English rugby if nothing else. The reasons for this are twofold. One: I am the man for the job, without question. Two: there is strong talk of you drafting in a *foreigner*. And an *Aussie* one at that!!!

That, with respect, Mr. Ritchie, is an odd prospect. Someone from Australia? The other side of the globe? A country farther away than any other? Apart from New Zealand? (Not sure why I made that last one a question when it was just a little factual correction of the previous question. Actually, I could've just replaced the question mark with a full stop, negating the need for this embracketed bit, making the quick letter that bit quicker to write. Oh well, you live and learn.)

The thing is, Ian, Australia is literally *miles* away. While that doesn't pose any practical or logistical problems in this day and age, what with the advent of aeroplanes and the ability to move to another country, the point is that Eddie Jones does not have an English heart. It is many years since we sent one of his criminal grandpas over there to start a family. Edward's genes are sufficiently diluted to make him very much un-English. So therefore, he *doesn't care* about the state of English rugby.

Not to mention the likelihood of bringing bad Aussie habits to the England squad. Who's to say he won't just spend his time feeding them barbeque food on the beach and drinking Foster's lager when he should be coaching? He'll probably have them playing cricket. With kangaroos. These are real risks that I seriously don't think you should be taking.

Instead, you are after a man who is English to the core. A man who breathes ruggers. A man that can galvanise his men, turn them from the hunted to the hunter, the little lemmings into the lauded lions. A man who can put the Great back into... England.

This is where I, a real rugby man who will arouse the roar once more, come in.

No doubt, you will want a man with exceptional experience and proven success in both playing and managing in the game of rugby. Well, let me tell you right now that I have no experience in either. But DO NOT, for the *life* of you, throw this letter away at this moment. That would be an awful thing to do as a human being, but more so, a terrible mistake, for I have so many other qualities so perfect for this role.

Besides, it's not quite true to say I have *no* experience in playing. I did once partake in a game during my high school years, and I did, in fact, score a try, albeit a consolation one as we were already 52 points down. And it was a bit of a fluke anyway. But what it did do is to set the groundwork for a love that has blossomed like pretty blossom blossoming on a lovely blossom tree and is now the pure *lust* I feel for rugby today. Literally, I want to make love to it. I just can't find a way to actually do so. The closest way I can think of is to manage the national team. (Please rest assured that I absolutely do not want to make love to all the players, no matter how attractive some of them may be; it's the concept of the game I lust after, not the big, strapping, physically magnificent sweating men that play it in their tight little shorts, all so tempting as they cuddle up in a scrum.)

What a lack of actual experience has given me is years and years and years of time to study rugby inside and out. I know rugby better than you know your daughter (if you have one). Certainly more than *I* know your daughter. I know it inside and out, all its intricacies in all their glorious detail. (I'm still talking about rugby.) There's no way of expressing my knowledge within this letter – you will just have to see for yourself when we meet and chat about the game. Trust me, you will be incredibly impressed – and probably *want* me to meet your daughter!!! (I will only agree if she is of age – I do not want any horrible unfounded rumours flaring up that could incriminate either of us on some level. I wish for no controversy, only to get on with making my rugby team great again.)

One of the very first things I learnt about rugby is that it is bloody rough. How silly, it seems to me, for 15 men (I *think* that's how many you have in a team) to take on another 15 men, only to fight over a ball that's not even a proper ball. Why is it not round? I do prefer my balls to be a little more spherical.

And why do some players allow their ears to become so knackered? They call them 'cauliflower ears', I'm told. Now, I'm all for advocating getting vegetables into us as part of a healthy diet (essential for creating athletic superstars, after all), but what is the point in *looking like* one? Do they crave intimacy from people and hope that someone will start nibbling them? I don't get it. So the first thing I'll be doing as Head Coach is to make it mandatory for players that insist on playing in the scrum to wear ear muffs. Good, furry ones that firmly connect to the head. It is for their hearing safety and to maintain their good looks should they have them. It could also be quite a cool fashion statement if marketed right.

The overall goal, of course, is to bring back the glory days. Since winning the World Cup in 2003, I have studied rugby hard, scientifically, looking at every aspect on an intricate level to work out what the perfect player looks like in each position and how they collectively make the ultimate team machine. The results are thus:

I will require seven men built like robots (the massive kind) and eight dancers (the Louis Spence kind).

"Robots?" I hear you exclaim. *"Dancers?!"* Yes, robots. Yes, dancers. For you see, games and pastimes evolve over years. Once upon a time, rugby would not have been rough. It has *evolved* to *become* rough. And maybe it will go back again. That's what happened to football. Look at the pansies that play that now!!! Yet see how more popular it is than it has ever been before.

I accept that the toughness is a part of the draw. That is why I want men like robots. Not actual robots. That would likely go against the laws of the game. Plus I doubt scientists have even invented the type that could react to sporting situations within a given match. I mean men the size of which we've never seen before. Muscled like gorillas. Aggressive like possessed hyenas, but with less humour. *Those* sort of men. I will create them, either from the existing bunch we have if they are up for it or to be recruited and built.

The dancers are the ones who are going to change the game forever. Where football has thrived is in the skill of the game. It's far beyond rugby, as much as it hurts me to my core to write that. Gone are the toughies like Vinnie Jones. He'd get nowhere near the twinkle-toes of Ronaldo now, would he? And so for rugby to finally triumph over football, we need to bring the game up to football's level of sublimity. That's what my dancing boys are going to do.

Dancing has an air of class about it, a sophistication and grace not seen in other arts. Speed, timing, co-ordination, accuracy… all essential for producing fabulous pieces of dance that people pay money to be enthralled by. If I can recruit the country's top dancers, get them on to my training fields and teach them the wonderful game of rugby, can you see the likes of 20-stone Will Skelton of Australia getting anywhere near Anton Du Beke?! Sure, we'll break a few of the little'uns on the way to achieving our inevitable success, but the collateral damage is absolutely worth it.

The game will not know what's hit it! It will be like rhinos against ferrets! And the ferrets will win! Hey, we'll even create a dancing version of the Hakka, really camped up, for when we're up against the All Blacks – can you imagine their angry faces?!!! *I can't wait!!!*

I just *know* you're as excited as me now! And so you should be – these are very exciting times coming up with me at the helm.

And if you are concerning yourself with my lack of actual experience in the game, think of this: David Cameron is managing a country, and one of the most important countries in the world. How many other countries has he managed before? None. Absolutely none.

I think I can look after a few boys prancing around a patch of grass.

I am so looking forward to hearing back from you. Please do not go Oz – **go me**.

Yours sincerely,

Sam Broadley

Sam Broadley

█████████

Ipswich
Suffolk

█████████

12th April, 2016

Dear Sirs,

I am writing to formally apply for the currently available position of **Director General** of the British Chambers of Commerce.

I can't begin to explain to you how excited I was when this job became available, but I will try nonetheless: like, *really* excited. It's the one I've been waiting for because I love you.

When John Longworth publicly entered the debate concerning the forthcoming EU referendum to give his personal views, it hurt me because it damaged the reputation of the BCC, whom I adore. But equally, I was bloody happy! And you will be, too, once you finish reading my application. You really will!

I can't actually believe that old John was daft enough to express his opinion on Brexit knowing full well that the BCC's stance on the topic was one of total neutrality. What a silly man. I think we should rename him 'John Long*UN*worthy'! And I mean by deed poll.

It just goes to show that, really, he never had the intelligence to be able to handle the job of Director General in the first place. With his history of working with the supermarket Asda, I would suggest he ought to go stack some shelves. (I have done that exact job during my youthful years for a rival firm called Tesco, but I knew even back then that I was better than that and destined for far greater things, ideally with the BCC (always loved you).

199

It is so difficult, though, to keep one's opinions to oneself, particularly when in a position of great influence. I mean, it would be fair to say that I have a massive impact on people's lives and their individual decisions, but I would never let that incredible power of persuasion I possess to get in the way of winning the position of Director General.

An example of the power I have within me in this way might be when recently, I told a group of strangers in a park that I passionately believe that England manager Roy Hodgson should bring Paul Gascoigne out of retirement for the forthcoming European Championships, not only for his incredible skill with a football, but to get all the players drinking before a match to relax them so they could play without the fear that so consumes them.

It's a fairly ludicrous suggestion (although a small part of me feels it might be the right approach – nothing else has worked), but it was another little test of my persuasive powers, and to say it was a success would be a deplorable understatement. They were whooping and cheering over the idea! I was hailed as a revolutionary! They wanted to start a social media campaign glorifying my name! I stopped them (with my power) because it's not about me.

These are ordinary people leading ordinary lives, yet I was basically able to control their minds such is the power of communication I have. But I would never abuse my God-given power to actually meet with Mr. Hodgson himself and persuade him to follow that path because he would *definitely* do it, and it would end in disaster, ridicule and, no doubt, a further significant decline of Paul Gascoigne. I couldn't have that on my conscience.

I sometimes think I should start a cult, though. I could own everyone. But no, I don't wish to use my powers for evil, only to serve you gorgeous people at the BCC and our wonderful group of 92,000 businesses. But only if I can make a significant difference to all concerned.

I've thought long and hard for many years about what I would do to encourage more companies to sign up when I become DG of the BCC (I feel a rap coming on – *Yo, I'm the Daddy DG of the BCC, come join us homies and give your business to me!*). Basically, I'm a business expert, of that there is no doubt. Right from my days of selling so-called chocolate seeds to thick children right through to my property-developing work of today where I ruthlessly target the elderly and infirm, I have earned impressive sums of money, literally hundreds, whilst doing good.

So this solid foundation of business knowledge I have developed and undoubted money-making acumen will be a springboard from which I can persuade business-owners to join us on our great quest to unite businessmen and -women and thrive where other countries fail. I want the good members of our wondrous BCC to be successful, for their companies to flourish so they can provide for their families, create jobs, build the economy and make Britain great again. And for them all to give me 10% equity in their businesses, obviously, as their mentor and hero.

I think I ought to mention the EU referendum as it's quite the topic at the moment, particularly in the context of this job for which I'm applying. It is such a complicated subject and one that is so hard to get around one's head. So as individuals, we each have a duty to listen intently to all the arguments on both sides of the debate and systematically weigh up the evidence to make a decision. Or just save all that effort and guess.

I for one will be doing neither. I ought to tell you that I will be voting to leave the European Union based on a single point close to my heart – I went for the job of President of the EU and they didn't even interview me. Just for that episode of incredible disrespect, I want a divorce, regardless of any dire national consequences.

Naturally, as a passionate Brexit man, I will most certainly be publicly campaigning to leave the EU. But before you shout, "HYPOCRITE!" and screw my letter up, I will be doing so far, far more subtly than our old friend (foe) John did when he stood on a stage and just blurted out that we should go. For me, my method will be far more subliminal. It's impossible to describe by written word how I will do this, but if your opinion is currently to remain in the EU, it will be reversed after my interview, but you will have no idea how because we won't even have discussed it!!! (Or so you will think…)

Listen: don't let the fear of me being able to manipulate your mind put you off interviewing me – I promise not to let you hand me your bank details! (Seriously, unremember your card PIN before I arrive – I can't trust myself.) We will have a delightful discussion before you accept me as your new Director General and I can rule the business world!!!

Yours sincerely,

Sam Broadley

Sam Broadley

██████████

Ipswich

Suffolk

████████

27th June, 2016

Dear Mr. Greg Dyke,

I am writing to formally apply for the position of **England Manager**.

This is my third time applying. The first in 2000, second in 2012. And now again. (Please check your records for my previous letters (I'm even better now than I was then.).)

To reiterate, this is my *third attempt*. Two rebuffs, two bad decisions, two managerial failures...

SO WHEN ARE YOU GOING TO LEARN AND TAKE NOTICE?????!!!!!

I look forward to hearing from you.

Yours sincerely,

Sam Broadley

Sam Broadley

████████████

Ipswich

Suffolk

████████

28th June, 2016

Dear Messrs Cameron, Corbyn and Dyke,

I feel it's important to clarify that bit above. Yes, this letter is addressed to you, David, and you, Jeremy, and you, Greg. All three of you. (I have sent you each a copy as I couldn't guarantee one would read it and pass it on to the next, particularly you squabbling politicians. You know who you are.)

'Cameron, Corbyn & Dyke'. Sounds like a solicitors' firm, doesn't it? Or a comedy act. Probably more likely the latter.

Anyhow, why am I writing to you all? Why have you each received identical letters? Why on Earth would I send the same letter to the Tory and Labour leaders and the Head of the Football Association? Simple: there are three jobs going. And I want them all.

So please could you consider this my formal application for the currently available positions of **Prime Minister**, the soon-to-be-challenged role of **Leader** of the Labour Party as well as the real poisoned chalice, that being **Head Coach** of the England football team.

Absolutely ridiculous! That's what you might think. Well, absolutely not, my friends. Just listen. Or, more accurately, read…

You see, what's happened here this last week, boys, is that the country has lost faith in itself. Where we were all once as one, there is now division. Where there was hope, there is only despair. Great Britain is a broken Britain. England's brilliance has all but crumbled into a million feeble pieces.

Actually, reading that bit back, it's not quite accurate. Your lot, David, and your lot, Jeremy, were *always* divided. You bloody *hate* each other! Which is not very nice! And to say there is only despair is not true because there are more than 17 million Brexiteers *oozing* hope! Thoroughly reeking of the stuff! (Apart from the ones who really regret voting Leave, but that's their stupid fault; if they can't tick the box they actually want to tick, they don't deserve to be ticking at all.) And as for England's brilliance, when was that?! Certainly not last night. Iceland! Goodness me. And don't say "1966" because that doesn't count! It was ages ago. Before the EU even existed! In its current format, at least.

Basically, what I'm saying is that this country is not what is should be. Was it ever? That's up for debate. All I know is that we're on the precipice of a disaster of epic proportions (like when you nearly lost your daughter in a pub, Dave) and we need a bloody hero to save the day.

This is where I, a people-rescuing, nation-saving, global-galvanising, crisis-crunching, situation-salvaging, disaster-dashing, mess-mashing, mass-motivating, fan-amassing, humble hero of all the heroes across all of time, come in.

So I'm applying for these jobs to save the day. And possibly the world. It is my duty.

So how will this work? How can I do all three jobs? Well, let's briefly take each in turn. (And it will be brief, relatively speaking; I'm sure each of you doesn't want to hear about the intricacies of roles that don't concern you. Why would you? Well, because you need to know there's no conflict of interest, for starters; that would be awful.)

For you, Dave, you're definitely off to pastures new. I thank you for your efforts as Prime Minister and the dignity that beheld you upon your declaration of exit because of Brexit. Well played, Sir. And it's now time for someone like myself, someone fresh, energetic, handsome and well capable of hitting the despatch box with the sort of panache to excite a country. To lead a country. To *own* it.

Talking of the despatch box, Jeremy, you're probably wondering who would be up against me in battle at Prime Minister's Questions on a Wednesday morn. Why, me of course! Well, I'll have to when I'm Labour Leader – it couldn't be anyone else! The way I see it is that as Leader of the Opposition, I'd put a question to the Prime Minister from one of my supporters from the general public (I like that you do that instead of asking your own questions; I'm not sure if it's a way of engaging your followers or you just can't think of any of your own, but it works). Once delivered, I'll quickly run round to the other side and offer my Tory retort. It's then a return to the Left to scoff at the apparently shabby answer, only to hop back to the Right to hurl some abuse at my Labour-loving self. And on it goes, back and forwards like a game of one-man tennis.

To bring you in, Greg (because you're probably wondering what the hell this has to do with you and the England football team), such leadership qualities, the ability to debate with such ferocity and success, the talent I will demonstrate for engaging others, the tactical nous I will inevitably display in winning arguments in the Commons on every single visit, I mean, I really will inspire this footballing nation. Think about it: if I can win for *both* teams in Parliament, *one* team, the England team, will be easy-peasy!!!

To add, I'm a handy footballer myself, although not good enough anymore to play for England (well, I thought I wasn't until last night's debacle). When a manager can play the game himself, he earns the respect of the fans. So to make Parliament even more exciting with me running the place, I will be entering the House on my debut appearance with a football, MPs from all sides seated and ready to cheer, and I'll be doing keepie-uppies and all sorts of tricks! That'll get 'em going! What a great way to *positively* engage our public in politics!

Actually, I've just thought of this: I mentioned the despatch box antics for Prime Minister's Questions being like a game of one-man tennis, didn't I? Well, I'm so good with a football that after I have asked the first question as Labour Leader, I am going to throw the ball from one despatch box to the other, sending it through the air on a trajectory that gives me the perfect amount of time to run across, give a brilliant answer, just in time to head it back over, then leg it back to the Left, throw a verbal curveball at the Prime Minister, volley the ball back, rag it over to the Right, sling a witty insult… all without letting the ball hit the floor! Oh, it'll be so exciting! What a way to bring sports and politics together as one! And we all want that!

But who will win??! Well, obviously, I'm playing for both sides, as it were, so me. But I need to ensure *both* sides are victors, and I will cleverly do this in such a way that while the verbal forehands and backhands are traded and the magnificent ball-volleying show is in full flow along with a display of my wonderful athleticism as I shuttle-run between the boxes, the actual arguments, although forceful, sometimes aggressive and even degrading, will slowly and slyly evolve into eventual agreement between the two, and there will be rapturous applause from the benches as, for once, there will be full unity between the Prime Minister and Leader of the Opposition, at which point, I will catch the ball on my neck, let it roll down my back, coolly back-heel it into the crowd to give some unimportant back-bencher a souvenir, walk to the centre and give myself a hug of mutual respect.

The point is that people are sick of the *Punch & Judy* shows we've been subjected to for years in Parliament. Politics is serious business. There are conflicts all over the world, social crises in our own land, not to mention this EU stuff. It's time to start making these things right, and that's down to us politicians. We must put aside our differences, throw away the pantomime-style theatrics we see today and get down to running this country in a firm, assertive and steadfast manner. That's why I'll be making the metaphorical political football a reality and bringing dispatch-box soccer to the House.

Talking of soccer, Greg (I hate calling it 'soccer' – we're not American; I just didn't want to have repetition of 'football' in the last paragraph), what about last night, eh? Ugh! Iceland! The land of ice! (Actually, I was interested to learn that Iceland's winters are warmer than Britain's; I wonder who chucked in that red herring).

(Dave, please feel free to excuse yourself from this next bit as I'm going to be discussing football with Greg. I know you say you support either Aston Villa or West Ham depending on how tired you are, but I don't think you're a true fan of the game like us. As for you, Jez, you're an Arsenal fan, but you are welcome to join in if you so wish.)

Every time England reach the finals of a major tournament, our hearts rule our heads and we cling to any scrap of evidence to believe we can win the thing! And then we are shocked when we get knocked out by a nation with a population small enough to fit in my shed as long as I've left the windows open!

It hurts so bad. We are all just disillusioned with our country. Time and again, managers come in, fail, go; come in, fail, go. It's got to change. We want someone who, yes, is a football man through and through, but not a yes-man. He's got to be a maverick. An eccentric. Someone who's not scared to rip up the rule book (metaphorically, not the laws of the game; we'll never win that way) and mix it up like a... cement mixer. And that man is me.

I must quickly say, Greg, that I apologise for my previous letter addressed to you dated 27th June. Although technically an application letter, it was rather 'to the point'. Concise, but not in a good way. I just felt emotional and frustrated that the FA haven't previously truly considered me as a viable option, and I've had to watch the country's footballing fortunes suffer as a result. Be in no doubt, though, that the letter was indeed a serious request for you to go and review my previous applications. I strongly urge you to do so. When you see what this country has missed out on, you will smack yourself on the forehead. Much like Joe Hart did, the clown.

To return you to direct proceedings, Jez and Dave (you sound almost like an '80s pop group!), can you see what I'm doing here? Can *all* of you see it? I've never seen a week like it where the country is on its knees in this way. It's going to the dogs. You're quitting, Dave. Woy has gone, hasn't he, Greg? Jezza, you're clinging on like Mustafa, and although I would have liked to see you survive, there's at least going to be a leadership challenge, for which you'll no doubt stand.

And so will I, if you'll support me. But don't see me as competition, even though I am. See it as a good thing for the Labour Party. I want your job, but I'm with you, Jeremy. I love what you stand for.

(And you, Dave; don't get jealous, I'll come back to you.) But with so many people trying to oust you, it is only right that someone else steps in, and for everyone's sakes, including yours, that man needs to be me. But I want you to know that you are my number-one choice for my number-two. A demotion, yes, but you will be my rock and I will be yours.

David, I love the Tories. With so much hatred surrounding the Brexit campaigns and the subsequent results, the party just has to bring in someone neutral to take things forward, rebuild relationships and mend the Tory family. I truly am the only man who can do that. What I need from you is to put my name forward as an official candidate. There's no time to waste by meeting with me, chatting and all of that because it has to be sorted by Thursday. Just chuck my name in the hat and I'll take care of the rest. Let *that* be your legacy instead of having, just as Woy did in his own little way, lead us out of Europe. (There's no real risk for you anyway because you're off so what do you care?)

Greg, please read my first two applications. It is absolutely imperative you do. In these times of political turmoil, people turned to our football superstars to bring joy into their lives. They were tremendously let down. We cannot and must not allow this to ever happen again. I bloody love football. I know it inside-out. I have the talent to make good things happen and the personality to bring it all together. Plus it's only a part-time job so it'll be easy to fit in around running the country and the Opposition.

One extra little thing relevant to you all: you need to know that although I am naturally a lefty, and a very gifted lefty at that, I am equally capable on either wing, and actually incredibly influential and exciting. I can just adapt superbly to either flank. This is great for us all!

Chaps, this is a lot for you to take in. I understand that, really I do. No-one has ever dared to even consider trying to run two opposing political parties, a country's government and its international football team before. Especially all at the same time. But I strongly believe this is the only way to mend Badly Broken Britain.

No-one cares anymore about the different things parties are supposed to stand for. No-one wants to see the squabbling, the fighting, the arguing, the slurs. They're fed up with a football team that underachieves to such a degree that a bunch of ice-dwellers can beat us.

We are in desperate, desperate need of a comer-togetherer. *I* am that comer-togetherer.

This is our last chance. Let us seize the might of the challenge. Let me rule this great country under a Broadley monopoly that will unleash greatness upon my people of Britain.

I look forward very much to meeting all of you to discuss how we implement this thing. Hell, we could go out on the lash together! Such exciting times.

Yours sincerely,

Mr. Sam D. Broadley

PS: I expect I'll be on a stamp soon.

4th July, 2016

Dear Mr. Broadley,

On behalf of Greg Dyke, thank you for your letters regarding the England Senior Team Manager position. Greg has asked me to respond to you.

Our defeat to Iceland and exit from Euro 2016 was obviously a bitter disappointment to us all.

The performance was nowhere near the standards required in the knockout stage of a major tournament and far below the level we aspire for England. It was a huge let-down to the many thousands of fans who followed the team so passionately and loyally, not just in France but through qualifying as well.

Roy Hodgson's decision to step down from his role along with the other members of his coaching staff is the right decision and we support it. Clearly, we need to change to improve if we are going to achieve our ambitions in the years ahead. What has stood out has been the magnificent support given to us from the stands. At every single match, England fans were incredible and never stopped singing.

Our young squad will be better for the experience and the passionate support our supporters have given them will encourage them to want to do better in future tournaments.

Rest assured, we will consider everything that has gone into this tournament and ensure we learn the lessons. Work is already underway with our CEO Martin Glenn, Technical Director Dan Ashworth and David Gill to ensure we manage the process of appointing a new England Manager and thank you for your application. These are not easy decisions but we will take the appropriate time to get it right.

We are confident that our investment in Coach Education and Sports Psychology in the National Football Centre at St. George's Park, which started two years ago, will bear fruit in the coming years and the success of our development teams gives us confidence that this will happen.

Thank you for taking the time to contact the FA.

Kind regards,

Yours sincerely,

Office of the Chairman

WEMBLEY

Sam Broadley

Ipswich
Suffolk

24th September, 2016

Dear BBC,

I am writing to formally apply for the currently available position of **Judge** on *Strictly Come Dancing.*

So I'm writing to a panel asking to be on a panel. Isn't that funny?! (That only works assuming it's more than one person (a panel) choosing the next Judge.)

I'm relaxing at home in my pants one day after a particularly frantic game of *Just Dance* on my Nintendo Wii when suddenly the news breaks: 'Len is quitting *Strictly*'!!!!! Literally the biggest shock exit since Brexit. Maybe even on a par. It was certainly bigger than David Cameron quitting the country. I think I speak for the nation when I say I don't care for him like I do Len.

Len leaving *Strictly* feels like the show cannot go on (despite the old adage, *The show must go on*). But the show must go on. Even though Len leaves a hole bigger than that which would've have been left in the floor by Russell Grant if his suspension wires had snapped that time. (Such acrobatics from the great(-sized) man!)

But for the show to go on, how on this mighty Earth are you going find someone to fill his Nueva Epocas? (That's a brand of quality dance shoe, you'll know.) It's obvious you'll require a man with extreme charisma, a catchphrase (like Len's ever-so-clever-and-witty "SevEEEEENN!"), phenomenal knowledge of dance moves and actual dancing talent to match. Probably some brilliant put-downs wouldn't go amiss either.

This is where I, a delicious, delectable and dashing dancing delight, come in.

And *damning*. I really ought to add that. Because you need some of those put-downs I mentioned. It makes for beautiful television, even when it ruins a contestant's life. An example of what I might come up with from behind that desk if I were there for the forthcoming series would be, "Oi, Ed! Balls by name, *no balls* by nature! Grow a pair, son!" And that would be a reference to his lack of courage on the dancefloor rather than any absence of a bulgy shape within the central region of his sparkly lycra trousers.

That's just an example off the top of my head. I wouldn't necessarily use it (although it is rather excellent so I might save it should the scenario arise!). It's just important for you to see what I'm capable of conjuring up. Sometimes, these celebs need bringing down a peg or two, particularly those in politics.

It actually upsets me that celebrities are the contestants on this show. Do they really need the publicity and money? Nope. Well, maybe one or two of them; the desperate has-beens. But wouldn't it be lovely for people who have never had a chance at making it big to be given a go? People who have honed their prancing to perfection?

Actually, I'm thinking very much of myself here, in an unselfish sort of way. You see, I really am a truly unbelievable dancer. Really extraordinarily good. And I don't say that lightly. Obviously with a base level of natural God-given talent, I have built up my abilities over many years, since being legally allowed to drink, in all manner of styles.

I've worked the 'floors in clubs of the night variety up and down the land. Across Europe and, indeed, the globe. It's always the nightclubs in which I express myself. It just feels so good for my glorious soul to be in that environment where I can be appreciated by party-goers lapping up my magical moves to hard-hitting club music. Honestly, you should see me. It's sublime viewing, I'm sure. The times the 'floor has cleared for me once my shapes begin to appear from nowhere. They have to make way because I'm akin to quantum physics – it's like I'm in two places at once such is my speed!!!

People sometimes just stand on the sidelines aghast; watching, pointing and laughing at me. But it's pointing in wonderment and laughing with pure joy at what they are witnessing, I can tell you. I just rock the 'floor. I *own* the 'floor. (A nightclub owner nearly signed the deeds of his place over to me once.)

And the amazing thing about me is that it doesn't matter what music the DJ throws my way, I can make *any* dance genre work. Think of any of the songs you might get in the Ibiza clubland and I can make anything fit it. Fandango or foxtrot, samba or street. Even ballet.

I think it's fair to say that alcohol does aid my sublimity, and maybe that's why I chose the clubs as the establishments in which to build my repertoire. It just takes the edge off my pre-dance nerves and loosens up my limbs. In fact, the more I drink, the looser I get, the more self-belief I ooze and the quality and size of my performances increase! If you can imagine a drunk, male ballerina gliding and twirling through the air to some hip-hop hits, occasionally throwing in some scintillating salsa and ballroom blitz... It really is a sight to behold at times.

I was thinking about the use of alcoholic substances during *Strictly* performances, actually. I haven't seen the rulebook but I would assume there's nothing to say that it's not allowed, although I suspect that no-one actually does due to the immense professionalism of the programme and all its performers. But for me, it's absolutely vital. It makes me *more* professional. Certainly more entertaining, which is surely what the show is all about.

You're probably wondering what the relevance is of whether or not I'd be allowed an intoxicating beverage or two pre-show; I'll be the judge, after all, not the dancer. Well, yes and no. And this is where I will bring something different to *Strictly*, something not seen before, despite the wonderful array of outlandish judges you've had on your panel.

You see, I've talked of my ability to throw the put-downs to shoddy contestants. That is necessary. They need to know they're an embarrassment to their families. Plus it's hilarious. But I see a real top-quality judge being one who will criticise fairly, but then they *must* be able to demonstrate how it *should* be done. And *this* is where I can shine. So if Balls's ballroom is a shocker, Broadley can step up to the plate. Not to *replace* him, just to show him how I am so much better and allow him to aspire to be as good as me. Probably to *be* me, truth be told.

Taking this method does three things. First, as above, it shows the contestant how it should be done; second, it breaks down their egos, which is so important, because if there's one thing I can't stand, it's over-confidence; third, what magnificent entertainment for the audience and watching millions!!!

I am a proven mover. A celebrated shape-maker. A real discotheque delight. It seems unfair, therefore, not only for me but the entire *nation*, that I have yet to entertain the... nation with my sensational skills. It would be unforgivable for me to go through life and the public at large miss out on me. I could cry at the thought.

Let me make it clear: my job is judge. That is my primary role. But I am a natural performer and you will not be able to stop me from getting up there and showing people the extent of what I can do. And nor would you *want* to stop me. You will actively encourage it!

A show, no matter how successful, *must* continue to evolve and improve. I am the man you need to take *Strictly* to the next level, a level incomprehensible to the naked… brain. I really will waltz it.

One final thing to plant in your wonderful little dancy, prancy minds… I am considering persuading you to have a judging panel of just *one* and *taking away* the public vote. Obviously, I will be the one remaining judge. It's not a power thing, I just think it's the fairest way of judging. My ego, unlike the celebrities', does not even come into it. If we run with this new format, I will be known forthwith as

JUSTICE BROADLEY: JUDGE, JURY AND EXECUTER.

(Executer, not Executioner, meaning I will execute the dance-moves for the rubbish contestants, not kill them; I'm a tough judge, but I don't believe in capital punishment for bad performances.)

I look forward to hearing from you very soon. In the meantime, I'm off to climb on the sink and practice my tap!!! (Just a little joke there.)

Yours sincerely,

Mr. Sam Broadley

PS: As for my catchphrase, you'll like it. Upon judging a contestant harshly and having to show them how it's done, I'll step up to prepare, kick my legs up in the air and declare……… "If anyone can, Sam can-can!!!!!"

12th October, 2016

Dear Sam,

Thank you very much for your letter, we are always grateful to hear from our viewers.

As you may appreciate, we receive a high volume of mail into the *Strictly* office, which can sometimes take a while to process, so I am sorry for the delayed response to your letter. I can assure you that we take all comments on board and your letter has been passed on to the appropriate people.

Thank you for applying for the new judge position, unfortunately it is too early to even think about who will take over from Len!

Thank you for taking the time to write to us, we hope you continue to enjoy the programme!

Kind regards (and keeeeep dancing!)

The Strictly Come Dancing Team

2nd November, 2016

Dear Sam,

Thank you very much for your letter, we are always grateful to hear from our viewers.

As you may appreciate, we receive a high volume of mail into the *Strictly* office, which can sometimes take a while to process, so I am sorry for the delayed response to your letter. I can assure you that we take all comments on board and your letter has been passed on to the appropriate people.

We thoroughly enjoyed reading your letter and don't doubt that you would suit those Nueva Epocas.

Once again, thank you for taking the time to write to us and we hope you continue to enjoy the programme!

Kind regards (and keeeep dancing... if anyone can, you can-can, right?)

The Strictly Come Dancing Team

Sam Broadley

██████████████

Ipswich

Suffolk

███████

24th October, 2016

Dear *Top Gear* owners,

I am writing to formally apply for the currently available position of **Presenter** of *Top Gear*.

I'm not a mind-reader. I cannot know if you are mildly intrigued or outright excited by the potential the following pages have in store for you and where this letter could take *Top Gear*. But I must make you wait just a little because we really ought to spend a quick moment reflecting on what went before I came on the scene. (Reading that back, 'clairvoyant' would've been more accurate than 'mind-reader' because you're not reading this at the exact same time as I'm writing it so you're reading it in the future (for me), meaning I can't, at this exact moment of mine, read your minds; if you *were* here while I'm writing it, there'd be no point in me typing and I may as well just tell you to your face.)

There seemed to be quite a bit of press attention, I noticed, over how the vacancy came about. Chris Evans, the bespectacled, dull-ginger fellow (how important was that hyphen there?!) was given the job after months of speculation, during which time he outright denied he was up for the job. When it was finally announced, my first reaction was one of despair because he had *lied* to us. How could I ever respect a man who was so happy to have us on like that presenting what is the best show commissioned for television anywhere ever? (I understand the workings of flattery, and that was a blatant attempt of mine, as you'll well know.)

There may also have been a smidgeon of bitterness on my part, to be fair. I was desperate, absolutely *desperate*, to present this show, but I didn't get the job. Technically, it was mostly my fault, I suppose; I didn't give myself a very good chance because I was far too slow on the uptake in getting in my application, to the point of never writing it. I stalled at the start line and never recovered.

You'll remember that prior to Chris, of course, the incumbent of the position was a man called Jeremy Clarkson. He still is called that, to my knowledge. And why wouldn't he be? I don't think the crushing of his already questionable reputation warrants a name-alteration. 'Jeremy' is not a great name, admittedly, certainly not cool, like a 'Carlo' or 'Valentino' or 'Sam', so maybe that's a reason for a change by deed poll.

But that's all by the by. What we know is that this man, whom we shall call 'Jeremy', is an animal. Well, we all are in a sense, that is, we form a species among the several that make up the animal kingdom on Earth. But what I mean is that 'Jeremy' is violent like a non-human creature. You know, like a kangaroo or something. Basically, he likes to punch people. Could I have made that point more succinctly? Yes, probably.

I agree in principle with the official reason 'Jeremy' lamped that producer. It's unacceptable for any human, even an animalistic one, to be denied their basic right to eat. But there were probably other more diplomatic ways to go about it. Less violent. Like spitting at him. But he chose to go down that horrible and disrespectful road of fist-to-face discussions. It's totally unacceptable, even if he didn't get the sausage he so craved. (*Not* a euphemism so stop sniggering. I've no idea what he's into sexually, and nor do I wish to. (Violent dominance…?))

So to (eventually) bring us to the subject of *me* (which is quite important for an application letter I've written), the first point I'd like to make about myself is that I am not, generally speaking, a violent man. I'm not an idiot – I would *never* thump another person and be caught. It's just the wrong thing to do and my morals are everything to me. Remember that please, because no doubt that's one of the first things you're looking for in your future main man.

The next thing, of course, is presenting skills! My word, that *is* important! So… what can I offer in that department? Have I done television presenting before? Nope. But that doesn't matter. Evans has presented *loads* of stuff and he was still rubbish on *Top Gear* so that should not be a prerequisite.

I have been on television before; once on a game show where it was widely accepted that I was a huge hit (despite winning exactly nothing) and should've had my own spin-off; and another time when I was interviewed on the local news for a magnificent charity challenge I was involved in (see – I don't do everything selfishly, unlike your last two).

In terms of presenting, though, I've presented in other ways and proven to be rather brilliant. You'll want an example. An example of this is when I presented a presentation at sixth form. Boy, was I nervous as I stood up there with literally a dozen classmates locking their eyes on me and just me, waiting impatiently for me to present my idea for a business innovation.

As soon as I had awkwardly and squeakily got my first few words out (those words being something along the lines of, "Um, My Business Plan, by Sam Broadley" (imagine them being said by a mid-puberty-onset 13-year-old (I was actually 18; I didn't have late onset, it was just the nerves making me squeak))), something just changed within my brain. Suddenly, I turned into a man. And a bloody entertaining one! I was promoting an idea for a product to do with wind through the sunroof (I can't give away the actual idea in case you steal it), and the crowd were whooping and cheering and virtually handing me cash to go out and get it made!

It was magical! I had these people (and almost their money) in the palm of my hand. And I loved it. *That* is when I knew I was made for television. (I also have plans to bring that very product to *Top Gear* and present it to the public; I'll be very happy to give you a modest cut of all profits made.)

Now you're definitely sold on my presenting ability, what about my knowledge of cars? Is it any good? Well, I certainly have enough to get by, and even drive them. I know the difference between a Mini and a Maserati, for example (one's a sporty number, isn't it?).

Have I ever raced cars before? No. But again, this should not result in an automatic failure for my application. You ought to remember that I once applied to be The Stig on your very show, and I also went for Formula One racing driver for Ferrari, and although I, rather disappointingly, didn't get either (why *didn't* I get the Stig gig? You never did reply…), it proves to you that there is no doubt in my mind of how much I have to offer on two, four or more wheels. Or even one (give me an engined unicycle and I'll show you some trickery!).

I'm extraordinarily brave and good and I'd love to have the chance to prove that to you by conducting a formal interview while sat in the driver's seat of a Morris Minor, tearing along some dangerous mountain-top track, you the passenger, asking me those all-important questions. You will be astounded at how talented I am in any given vehicle under such pressure. You just wait.

I noticed, by the way that Joey from *Friends* is intending to stay on as a co-presenter. Well, it's best I get this in early: no, he won't be. He was hilarious in that American programme, really funny, but you can't have someone that daft on a show about cars. Nothing at all against Joey, he comes across as a lovely man (if a little amorous), but he demonstrated in *Friends* that he doesn't even know his left from his right! You can't have someone that thick on *Top Gear*, not when we wouldn't know what side of the road he might end up driving on!

I've got my own ideas for sidekicks who I intend on approaching. One is Sir Bradley Wiggins. I like the idea of someone who just rides bikes everywhere presenting a car show. It's quite humorous, plus we can incorporate his bicycle into some outrageous sketches, no doubt, like racing against a Lada or something.

My other co-presenter will be Donald Trump. He probably won't have a job very soon and will be looking to repair his shattered reputation as a human being (which is what I *think* he is), and what better way to do that than on the world's most popular car show. Even if he somehow gets to be President, he won't mind popping over to the UK every week for some recording. Even if the Americans don't appreciate him taking time out from running their country, he won't care. And don't worry about his narcissism and undoubted attempt to take over the show – believe me, I'm a bigger deal than he'll ever be. He's lucky *I'm* not American.

I've just thought of a great idea to launch our new *Top Gear* version. Gather all the press together in a field near an airport and wait for Trump's plane to fly low overhead, upon which Bradley Wiggins's bike will be strapped upright. Upon that will be me, holding on to the handlebars for dear life. As soon as the plane is at the right height and position over the meadow on its way to land, the bike will be released from its shackles and I will fly off, cycling through the air until I skilfully land on an ideally-placed jumping ramp, race up that ramp (probably using momentum alone by this point), somersault mid-air off the bike and land incredibly into the driving seat of a convertible Cadillac, before cruising off into the distance (or more accurately, to pick up Donald and Bradley from the airport). Imagine that!

The fact is that you need someone to drive this show back to the good old days. With me behind the wheel, I'll indicate right from the green light that success is on the horizon. I have the focus and brightness of a cat's eye at night. I never get tyred, and suffer exhaust-ion I do not, for I have an engine with endless capacity that will propel me to brilliance.

You've given Clarkson and Evans the boot, but you need clutch at straws no longer, for you've found your perfect man. Belt up, take your foot off the brake and let Broadley take you on a journey of joy. I am your key to conquering television once more. No more being stuck in a jam for *Top Gear* – it's a clear road ahead and Victory is our destination.

NOW LET'S REV UP THIS SHOW!!!!!

I look forward to meeting with you very soon upon a mountain of your choice.

Yours sincerely,

Sam Broadley

Sam Broadley

███████████

Ipswich
Suffolk

███████

6th December, 2016

Dear Channel 4,

I am writing to formally apply for the currently available positions of **Presenter** and **Judge** of *Great British Bake Off.*

I suppose the first thing I ought to say to you is this: congratulations on your coup! I think I speak for the nation when I say it's fantastic that a massive corporate outfit has poached a TV treasure from the publicly-owned monster that is the BBC. It serves them right for charging us money to watch their stuff; at least you just bore us with adverts. I can safely say they got their just desserts.

I say I speak for the nation, but actually there was a bit of an outcry, wasn't there?! Crikey, people are sensitive. "Oooh, I've gotta press number four on my remote instead of number one now!" Idiots. Some people just don't deserve the pure joy of watching hours upon hours upon hours of cakes baking in an oven.

And in fact, it appears to actually be those adverts of yours that are putting people off tuning up three channels. They can't bear the idea of being parted from their precious *Bake Off* for just a few minutes! But to be honest, people should be cutting down on sweet stuff in this obesity epidemic we are witnessing so they should see those ad breaks as a symbol for life.

I love cake. I really do. Honestly, any cake, doesn't matter what it is. As long as it's a big cake! Gotta be a BIG cake! And I'm not one for sharing my big cake, either. Why would I? Who seriously gives away chunks of something they love? If I was physically capable of baking a cake, I would eat all of it!

And it's this lust for the moist stuff that makes me perfect for the show. Talking of my lust, I ought to quickly mention my (to-be) presenting predecessors, Mel and Sue. My lust? No, there is none here. They're not for me. I don't just mean sex-wise; it's their style I don't appreciate. What do they offer the show? Just a load of innuendo, which I personally find very offensive indeed. But if that's what the public demand, I'm happy to forego my moral standing on such an issue and feed them all they crave.

So an example of some clever double-entendre I might offer is, "Oof, what succulent buns," or, "Mmmmm, that's a creamy filling," or, "Cor, I'd love to taste your flan."

There, I've written them. Now let's never speak of such filth again until filming day.

Now back to the proper bit of my application and what I can offer you at this exciting time as you take this strangely popular show into a new era. (One really does wonder what it is that is so exciting watching some people chucking random stuff into a bowl, mixing it all up, spend hours waiting for it to cook, then spending even more hours making it look pretty, only to look on nervously as some beardy, judgemental git (not Mary, the other one) coarsely takes a hunk out of their polished piece, only to tell them it ain't very nice.)

I can't be bothered to go and read back, but I *think* I hinted to you that I can't really bake. It's just not my specialty, mainly because I'm not particularly interested. What's the point when I've got a cake shop at the end of my road? But just because I can't *make* a cake, doesn't mean I can't *eat* a cake and *judge* whether or not it tastes good. Let's face it, those judges are basically glorified food critics, that's all. Anyone can do that. But not as well as me.

I'll be honest, I'm struggling to get excited about applying for this job. It's just a show and a format that makes my bones ache with boredom. But make no mistake, it doesn't mean I don't want it. I want it so bad it makes my bones ache. And when you inevitably meet me for the interview, I promise that *all* your bones will be aching for me. And I do mean all…

You'll have noticed that in the first line of my letter (by which I mean the first *after* the line with my name on it and all the lines of my postal address and the date I'm writing this and the bit where I wrote 'Dear Channel 4'), I stated that I am applying for **Presenter** AND **Judge**. You can nip through and check with Rachel Riley from *Countdown* if you like, but I can assure you that it amounts to *two* jobs within this letter as opposed to the conventional *one*.

But why? Am I hedging my bets in the hope that I get one or the other? If you think that, then you really don't know me very well at all, and that hurts. But not to worry, you soon will. (To clarify that bit, I actually want both jobs to be performed together, the advantage to you being that you don't have to fork out for additional staff unnecessarily, and the advantage for me being that I can indulge myself in both TV celebrity and power over the people, which would make me feel really good.)

But why would you go for me? What possibly puts me ahead of anyone else who might want to head up this cult-like television programme? Well, I'm glad you asked (without realising and via my own choice of words). Aside from my outstanding ability to taste and form opinions on any given foodstuff I encounter upon my glorious tongue, which makes me a perfect judge, I also have a truly incredible personality and charisma so perfect for television presenting, to the degree that it will draw tens of millions, maybe *hundreds* of millions, or even *billions*, from all the other channels across the world, enough for those stations to potentially close down just for the hour *Bake Off* is on, realising there is literally no point in airing while I am on the telly.

But although my astounding ability to draw people in is bloody impressive, it will not be enough to retain them without a top-notch show. You will find this difficult to believe when you meet me, and maybe I'm wrong, but I don't want to leave it to chance. So I am going to persuade you to overhaul the format of the show to keep our newfound followers. Ready?

We are going to combine *Bake Off* with two other hit Channel 4 shows: *Come Dine With Me* and *Gogglebox.*

Yes, we are. It will be a brilliant innovation for all three shows, but particularly *Bake Off*. I see it working along the lines of the *Bake Off* contestants actually being contestants on *CDWM* as well. So we'll see them have those weird meetings with one another round each other's houses before preparing meals using the *GBBO* format, you know, making some sort of pie and then some kind of sponge or whatever it is they make on that show. We get the edgy, nerve-wracking competitiveness of the baking, followed by the sitting round the table in the contestants' dining rooms and the subsequent living-room debauchery (it really is an odd show).

Meanwhile, the usual eclectic collection of *Gogglebox* people sit there in what I assume are their homes and watch this wonderful collaboration of two amazing shows in awe and excitement, or more likely, considering the type of contestants I intend on getting on this new almighty show, despair and disgust. The programme will cut to them intermittently to hear their typical offerings of commentaries on the baking/dining situations presented to them.

As for me, I will be the host for the show, presenting it brilliantly and interacting with the contestants while they're turning on the ovens and prancing about with their scones. As the judge, I'll obviously have to sit at all the dining tables round each of their houses so I can taste and judge what they have dished up. I know it might be awkward for the contestants, like inviting your boss round where you can't say what you really want all night, but I really am such good company at dinner parties that everyone will have a really good time, even when I tell them their dinners make me feel sick.

And I must insist also on being in the *Gogglebox* bit. This is the only of the three shows I actually like so it would be a shame for me to not be on it. So each time you cut to one of the living rooms of the *Gogglebox* lot, I'll actually be there as well, in all the houses, only in a listening capacity, but mainly making comments myself. I will allow others to speak sometimes, if only to ridicule them.

I think it's this latest quirk, me offering my comments about a show I'm actually *in*, that'll make this new merger of your best three programmes absolutely perfect. The cherry on top, if you will. Hey, maybe we could even get on *Countdown*!

I know I don't own the show and I'm only going to be the presenter and judge of *Bake Off* and so it is north of my pay grade to be making decisions on format, but it just goes to show how much I care about this British institution to want to go above and beyond. I just so desire for it to become so much better than it is now, for it to actually be interesting. It's about job satisfaction – I need it to

232

be at least a little bit exciting to entice me to stay in the role long-term. I can't just be standing there waiting for things to cook. I'm entertaining but I can't keep it going for hours. So by amalgamating this trio of shows, you get a fresh format and three audiences for the price of one (as well as billions more new viewers, basically anyone who's got a TV). *And* you can guarantee the longevity of me and my fabulousness. That is magnificent news for you.

Something else you will get from me, by the way, is loyalty. It doesn't matter if another channel gets the rights for *Bake Off* in the future, I would never leave Channel 4. That is not to say I approve of the decision made by Mel, Sue and Mary. To stay loyal to the BBC is just daft when they could be joining you lot for bigger bucks for doing the exact same show! And not even the same *length* of show once you account for the adverts! Less work, more money… who wouldn't do that?! Absolutely mental.

My friends at Channel the Fourth, I am the man you need and so desire. A presenter, a judge, a god of television. That's not me being over-confident, I'm just offering you a fact. And please know that I'm humble with it, which is yet another good thing to add to my impressive list of attributes.

Please contact me soon because I need to know well in advance whether or not I need to be devising some smutty filth for the show; I hate it so it takes me time to come up with that vileness.

Yours sincerely,

Mr. Sam Broadley

PS: I am, grammatically speaking, Mr. Perfection. Therefore, I will be insisting on adding a hyphen between '*Bake*' and '*Off*'. This is non-negotiable. And possibly again between '*Great*' and '*British*'. I haven't decided on that one yet, though; I need to check it with Stephen Fry. Bye.

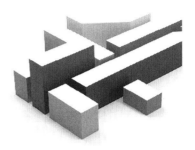

16th December, 2016

Dear Sam,

Thank you for writing to the Viewer Enquiries Department regarding *The Great British Bake Off*.

We would like to apologise for the delay in our response to your comments as we are currently experiencing a higher volume of enquiries than normal.

We appreciate that you took the time to contact us regarding this matter.

Please be advised that Channel 4 commissions or buys programmes but doesn't produce any in-house, so we don't have any access or contact with the programme-makers who are responsible for deciding who will judge and present this series on Channel 4.

We are sorry for any disappointment caused to you.

Please be assured that we have forwarded your letter to the programme-makers.

Nevertheless, please be assured that your interest in this programme has been logged and noted for the information of those responsible for our programming.

Thank you again for taking the time to contact us here at Channel 4 and for your interest in our programming.

Kind regards,

Scarlet Lewis

Channel 4 Viewer Enquiries

Sam Broadley

█████████████

Ipswich
Suffolk

████████████

8th March, 2017

Dear EON / MI6,

The name's Broadley, Sam Broadley: licensed to thrill your pants off!

I am writing to formally apply for the position of **Agent 007 James Bond.**

You'll have noticed that I'm writing not just to you but someone else as well. So EON, I'm writing to MI6 also, and MI6, I'm writing to EON in addition to you. There's a good reason for this, which is that I know Mr. Bond is for cinema and so it would make sense to apply directly to the production company as I am doing, but I want you good people at MI6 to have a look at how great I am and consider me to be a *real* James Bond. I think I can do both. So please read on, y'all, and get yourselves all excited!

Strictly speaking, the role of the world's most famous spy (which doesn't make sense because spies should be completely *unknown*) isn't actually available. But the fact is that rumours are flying around like bullets in a China shop full of Triads that Daniel Craig, the current incumbent, is to cease employment with MI6 (the fictional version, I assume) imminently having saved the world enough times for his liking.

Whether or not these rumours are true I cannot know. Only *you* know that (I'm talking to EON – unless, MI6, you have close ties with EON, do you, and are in the know?). What I *do* know is that I was born to play the role, both on screen *and* for real, and I am at the absolute optimum moment in my life to take it and crush world-enders everywhere! So if it is true that Craig is to hang up his Aston Martin, I need to be proactive in telling you that I am the man to lift it off its hook and drive it even better than he ever did.

Please note at this point that I am uncomfortable talking about myself. It's a British thing, I think. I prefer to let others speak of my greatness. But, alas, such are the requirements of a job application, I have no choice but to express the truths myself.

So you'll probably want to know a bit about me. Here are some things about me…

I'm a man. That's a prerequisite, I'm sure (although you never can tell with those equality idiots – they probably want a Janice Bond). I'm 36, a fantastic age to be taking on the world – not yet 40, but well old enough to know my way around. I'm in exquisite physical condition. Almost. And I'm an actor. An amateur one at present, but an actor nonetheless. Certainly professional in my quality. That gives me a huge advantage over non-actors.

Maybe I should elaborate on those things. Here are some elaborations…

Well, I can't really elaborate much on being a man, other than by claiming to be a very manly man. Which I am. Although when you learn of some of the roles I've played over the years, you may not quite believe that. But any effeminate vibes I give off upon the stage is testament to my acting ability by becoming someone I'm really not. But we'll come to that later when I elaborate, as promised, on my actorness.

As for my age, well, it's difficult to express how perfectly placed I am in terms of my maturity. As a boy, I was particularly immature in my attitudes and experience. I was naïve. I watched *Bond* films, the likes of Moore and Connery, and I never agreed with the concept of spies such as them interfering with criminal capers. I didn't feel it was their place, really. I believed in freedom of expression for individuals, so if some horrible git wanted to have a go at taking over the world, let them get on with it and see what happens.

But with years comes wisdom, and as I got older, I realised that bad people are bad, and when bad people are bad, bad things happen to non-bad people. And that's bad. Badness is not fair, so I became an advocate for goodness defeating badness.

And when I suddenly wanted Bond to win having developed this new and mature way of thinking, I realised that I needed to be him. This was around the time of Brosnan. He was good. And sexy. And so I set about emulating him during the years since. And then Craig. I sharpened my coolness, for example, which I already had a strong natural base level of, but I worked on it to hone that trait.

I also read up on spying. To become an expert in a subject, one must study one's butt off, and then one must put what one has learnt into practice to prove to one that one has got it. This one has. At 36, I have amassed such knowledge that you would think I already work for MI6. (I don't work for MI6, although there's no way you, EON, could know for certain if I do or don't; even parts of MI6 might not, so you, MI6 letter-reader, probably haven't seen my name, unless you are high up the chain and I *am* an MI6 spy (which I'm not, although I wouldn't tell you if I was, although I probably wouldn't be applying for a job I already had, unless it was to throw EON off the scent, which it isn't, unless it is, which it isn't…).

I have put in quite a lot of practice up to now to make sure I can spy well. An example of this is when I used my newly-acquired 'silent scaling suckers' to climb the outside wall of a block of flats to watch my mate fornicate with his new girlfriend through his bedroom window on the ninth floor.

I must stress that this was not for any sexually-motivated voyeurism reasons – it was just that he'd never had a partner before and it seemed unlikely so this was the only way to prove he was not lying to me. I'm happy to report that he was telling the truth. It was quite an impressive performance, actually, considering he'd never before had a girlfriend.

Now on to my physical condition. Generally, I'm happy with my physique. I'm a strong man and I look good. I mean, yes, there's an *incy-wincy* bit of chub in the odd spot, such as my tummy, chest, sides, back, upper arms, inner thighs, cheeks and chin, but honestly nothing you'd notice on camera.

But I don't want you to just take my word for it so I've included a couple of photographs of myself for proof of my 99% body quality. These were taken especially for you in the sea of Felixstowe, a tribute to that iconic shot of Craig in a like situation. You'll see for yourselves that there's very little difference between us. The only difference, really, is the colour of the sea – it's rather brown down in the 'Stowe. And bloody freezing so you'd better appreciate my efforts!

Now for my acting career. Well, I've played an array of roles down the years, a real variety. I am sometimes ever so camp on stage. I just love dressing up as a woman, usually in panto, putting on a load of make-up and prancing about the boards! But that is in no way a reflection of the real me; I'm only telling you to show the range of my performance skills, my ability to turn my hand to any role thrown at me.

And to prove it, I can tell you about the manly parts I've played. I once took on the role of a randy German sailor in a production of *Cabaret*, for example. I loved that part. I got to kiss girls and touch them (only by hugging, unfortunately). More recently, I was all over a woman in the toilets for everyone to see (I don't mean public toilets somewhere – the show was set in a nightclub restroom). Only last year, I played a suave estate agent pretending to own a country house in order to woo a sexy woman. I was a bloody charming liar! It was a shame, actually, because it was a farce and I ended up falling arse over head down some stairs in the name of comedy – not exactly becoming of a future Bond, but never mind.

What these experiences made me realise is that I am a natural performer and entertainer, and I am partial to the odd lustful performance with the ladies in front of any audience (although should my mother be there, this may well embarrass the both of us; luckily, *James Bond* is for cinema so our eyes will not meet when I take on the role). *Bond* films are obviously for the family, but I want you to know that when I take on the role, I am willing to go as racy as is necessary to enjoy triumphant success.

It's worth mentioning, in a modest kind of way, that I was a model once. Not on a major scale, admittedly, but a catwalk of any size is an opportunity to woo the ladies and strut my stuff. I feel uncomfortable saying it, such is my naturally humble personality, but I am unquestionably gifted when it comes to modelling. It's not just about appearing confident, handsome and oozing sex appeal; there's more to it. It's a *performance*. One needs to engage with the audience, excite them. I regularly enjoyed the sounds of wolf-whistles, screams and the lustful 'come-to-bed' eyes – almost always from women.

I'm only telling you about that because you need to know that I have a way with the public. They go out of their way to come and see me in whatever I do – even when it is flogging suits on a catwalk at wedding fayres. By transferring this experience to the big screen and all the publicity that goes with it, we really are on to a guaranteed winner!

Just to show you how seriously I am already taking my role as James Bond, I've taken the liberty to write a quick scene. It goes as follows:

> *Bond is in China hiding from the Triads, who are planning a coup of the Chinese Government. Looking inconspicuous, donned in a slick white suit, royal blue shirt and scarlet tie, 007 enters a bar and orders his standard Vodka Martini. He will insist it is shaken and not stirred. A highly attractive young lady, obviously drawn to the dark-haired Western man, approaches him at the bar and whispers in his ear. Bond smiles, and without pause, walks towards the stage to the karaoke. Despite the impending danger and his life under serious threat, Bond takes to the mic and sings* Do You Really Want to Hurt Me? *It really is a beautiful rendition. The Triads spot him from the back of the club. They can't help but listen to him intently, heads tilted, before snapping out of it and making a beeline for him. Bond sees the danger in advance, waits for them to get close to the speakers before screeching hard into the microphone, causing everyone to fall to the ground clutching their ears in agony. Bond makes good his escape.*

That was just a quick idea off the top of my head. You don't have to use it. It's just to point out that we could make use of my angelic singing voice as a way to innovatively develop the character and his range of powers. This I will do superbly.

I would like to firmly point out, though, that despite how much you might like my idea above, I have no interest in taking on a script-writing role. I very much believe my talents to lie on-screen so please do not consider me for anything behind the scenes.

To my production-company pals, I say to you this: should this really be Daniel Craig's farewell, as I believe it should, you have *got* to bring in someone who is off-the-scale amazing in every way. That someone is me. A lesser man does an injustice to the heritage of Bond and all the good he has brought to the world. I am the *only* man to take over. I will dominate the role. Revel in it. Own it. Save the world time and time again.

To my MI6 mates, I say to you this: you can see for yourselves the overwhelming evidence that I would take to spyship like Bond to a bird. All the skills I possess, my physical and intellectual stature, my ability to pretend to be other people… I am the perfect man. If you could build the perfect human spy, you would just build *me*. But no need – *I already exist.*

To both, I say this: come speak with me. We can make this thing happen. You'll be *even more* impressed with me in person than you undoubtedly are by this fabulously enlightening letter.

Meet me. I will not stir you, but I *will* shake you.

Yours faithfully,

Mr. Sam Broadley

PS to MI6: Please remember to *not* send a copy of your reply to EON. I know these mistakes are easily made, but my safety is of paramount importance to us all and so no-one, not even my soon-to-be employer, can know I work for you as well. *If* I do. Thanks.

PPS to MI6: You might be worried that by becoming James Bond and thus naturally becoming world-famous, it would make me unworthy of becoming an actual spy. But don't be concerned – no-one in their right minds would believe a pretend spy would be an *actual* spy as well! Impossible!!! What a clever ploy that would be!

PS to EON: I note that at some point since your emergence on the film-production front, you've successfully diversified into home energy supply. A commendable leap from what you know. I am not happy with my current provider so I'll be in contact again shortly, more privately without the prying eyes of MI6, to discuss my electricity and gas. Thanks.

EON

28th March 2017

Dear Sam Broadley

Many thanks for your letter dated 8th March 2017. We appreciate the time and effort that you took to write to us with your 007 Scene and Application.

Unfortunately we are unable to accept any unsolicited material. Eon Productions Limited and its affiliated company, Danjaq LLC, have a long standing policy of not reviewing James Bond material where they have not specifically commissioned its creation.

This is a policy borne out of the increasing number of infringement claims which plague the entertainment industry. It is a firm policy and one that will not be changed, no matter the number of pleas that are made. You should understand that we get many requests to review material each day and all of them are handled in the same manner.

You should also be aware that Danjaq LLC and Metro-Goldwyn-Mayer Studios Inc. control all film rights in the Ian Fleming James Bond novels, and own all copyrights and other rights in the 24 James Bond films produced to date. Accordingly, you should not attempt to exploit your ideas through any other source while it contains these protected elements.

Thank you very much for your interest in Eon Productions.

Yours sincerely,

Eon Productions Ltd.

AFTERWORD

Why is it called an afterword? I'm still writing words so it's not after all the words, is it? I suppose it is after *some* words.

Anyway, we're at the end of the book. Well, after the letters bit, anyway. When I've finished this so-called afterword, we'll *definitely* be at the end of the book.

So what have we learnt? Well, it's fair to say I didn't get a single job out of all the ones I applied for. And it may be true that I'm still stuck in a world of employment unbefitting of my potential. So am I a failure? Absolutely not.

For you see, I may not have got any offers, but it's only because the people who make the decisions on who gets them just couldn't open their minds widely enough to see that I was so perfect for the roles. I accept that, on the face of it, recruiting someone like me, an unknown, to any of the most powerful positions in the land will be seen by the wider world as foolhardy, reckless and downright ludicrous, with potentially horrendous consequences across the country and around the globe.

But perception does not always match reality, my friends. The *reality* is that I would have brought greatness to these positions. My radical thinking and incredible ideas would have overhauled any of those roles, the results being truly magnificent. (There's almost no point in me writing this – you've read the letters for yourselves now and you'll be as flabbergasted as I.)

I do, though, take great heart from my quest and draw boundless positives from my experiences. Although I was unable to persuade any of them to take me on, it's obvious I was not far off.

There's a reason Boris Johnson('s office) took me to the second stage of the selection process for Chief of the Met Police, and there's a reason the Queen replied to me in the manner she did (via her staff) for the same job. But they allowed the fear of a public backlash to get the better of them, despite the fact they *knew*, no doubt, that national opinion would flip in our favour in no time at all.

If you look at some of the other replies I received, several of them did not say, "Thanks, but no thanks". I can only assume, therefore, I was on the respective shortlists. Think back to my very first application, for example, that being for England Manager – a shortlist of three people was drawn up and *no mention* that I was not one of them. Why *wouldn't* they tell me I wasn't one of the trio after taking the trouble to write to me? So I *must* have been.

The same goes for *Bake-Off* Presenter – clearly, I was being seriously considered. No interview was forthcoming, so again, it can only be that they just didn't *dare* bring in this unknown whizzkid. Even for those jobs for which they couldn't be bothered to reply, they weren't rejections. If they were sure they didn't want me, they'd have sent me a letter saying so. It *must* have been that I was a credible candidate and my letters got them excited, but, just like the others, fear got the better of them.

And what about the reply from *Strictly*? There were actually two (*that's* how much they loved me), but in one they said they, quote, "don't doubt you would suit those Nueva Epocas." Don't doubt! *Don't doubt!* They had absolutely *no doubt* I was suitable for the job and *still* didn't give it to me!!! Absolutely amazing.

What none of these people realise is that they've let their country down. A simple "Yes" to bring in this magnificent applicant and their organisation, company or establishment and the world as a whole would've been lifted out of despair and into pure wonderment.

You'll have noticed there was no rejection from Eon in my most recent application, either. A little threatening maybe, but I think it's quite possible I could be the next James Bond judging by that letter so keep an eye out for me!

Remember that none of my effort, my tremendous effort, to win one of these roles has been for me. My sole goal in life is to inspire others. To inspire *you*. I'd hoped to do that through having a massive job, but not so. Not yet.

Now you've read about it, *you* can see how amazing my quest and I are. So be inspired. Go out there and achieve greatness. Never give up. Offer the world your fabulousness. Be the very best you can be in life.

If you could stay away from the big jobs, though, I'd appreciate it – it's hard enough to bag them without you lot wading in.

———